Praise

'This book is the go-to guide on the value of blockchain in enterprise scenarios and how to approach implementing a blockchain-based solution.'
— **Mark Russinovich,** Azure CTO and Technical Fellow, Microsoft

'Conor is a deep domain expert in Ethereum technology and has sketched a thoughtful map of the foothills of a global economic and social paradigm shift of mountainous proportions that will make previous paradigms look like molehills. This is an authoritative and inspiring account of how and why the disruptive technologies enabled by decentralized protocols – blockchain, cryptocurrencies, digital assets, NFTs, DAOs – will remake the world and bring far greater economic and political agency to the broad population.'
— **Joseph Lubin,** CEO and Founder, ConsenSys and Co-founder, Ethereum

'Only the most knowledgeable experts who are also gifted communicators can make complex things sound easy. Conor Svensson has that rare combination of skills. The book is not only an excellent read, but a very important one, too.'
— **Raoul Pal,** CEO/Co-founder, Real Vision Group and CEO/Founder, Global Macro Investor

'*The Blockchain Innovator's Handbook* is not only an essential guide for the novice and expert alike, it also provides a straightforward action plan for business leaders to get started and get results. It is a timely work that can help ensure you don't miss the next business revolution powered by blockchain.'
— **Todd McDonald,** Co-founder, R3

'*The Blockchain Innovator's Handbook* is not only a great blockchain ecosystem primer, but also a fantastic springboard into an innovator mindset.'
— **Marley Gray,** Chairman of the InterWork Alliance and Principal Architect, Microsoft

'This book is a very relevant read if you want to understand the current world and potential of the decentralised economy. Our behavior has been forever changed and you will need to adapt your business models, are you prepared?'
— **Mariana Gomez de la Villa,** Program Director Distributed Ledger Technology, ING

'*The Blockchain Innovator's Handbook* is an essential read. It not only provides a primer on blockchain technology and the many innovations that have emerged from it, such as cryptocurrencies, decentralised identity, NFTs and DeFi, but it also provides a pragmatic guide on how enterprises should approach its adoption to harness its full potential.'
— **David Palmer,** Blockchain Lead IoT, Vodafone Business

'*The Blockchain Innovator's Handbook* explains in depth the concept of blockchain in terms that are easy to understand and provides a comprehensive and practical guide for innovators who want to understand the journey needed to build solutions using blockchain.'
— **Susan David Carevic,** IT Officer, Carbon Markets and Innovation, Climate Change Group, The World Bank

'*The Blockchain Innovator's Handbook* provides breadth in its coverage of blockchain technology and terminology, and depth in the detail of finding and bringing a solution to market. Whether your innovation relies on blockchain or a completely different disruptive technology, Conor's step-by-step approach from exploration through to deployment will benefit both new and seasoned technology adopters alike.'
— **Daniel C. Burnett,** Executive Director, Enterprise Ethereum Alliance

'A comprehensive summary of blockchain's past, present and future. A useful guide for any executive looking to explore or integrate DLT and Web3 technologies in their organisation. Lots of useful learning tools, tips and strategies in an easy-to-understand format.'
— **Dr Naseem Naqvi,** President, The British Blockchain Association

'In his book, Conor has deftly crafted the 'go-to' blockchain survival guide, of particular value to the corporate innovator. Well researched and engaging, it quickly builds foundation knowledge, dispelling common myths along the way and ending with a robust toolkit to support the first exciting implementation opportunities.'
— **Alex Banks,** former Head of Innovation, NatWest Markets and CTO/Co-founder, Pet Proactive Insurance

'Decentralization and the democratization of innovation aligns incentives and creates an unstoppable flywheel to build communities and deliver new products to market with global reach at a much lower cost than ever before. *The Blockchain Innovator's Handbook* shares comprehensive insight and pragmatic guidance to position you and your business for the paradigm shift to blockchain networks, cryptocurrencies and decentralized finance.'
— **Shawn Douglass,** CEO and Co-founder, Amberdata

'Conor has taken a subject which is often misunderstood and laid it out in a very accessible and logical way. I was left feeling enthused about the extensive possibilities for innovation around blockchain and the future it brings. Very accessible and builds knowledge throughout.'
— **Adam Clarke,** CTO, Fnality International

The
Blockchain Innovator's Handbook

A leader's guide to understanding, adopting and succeeding with this disruptive technology

Conor Svensson

Rethink

*To my family – you are my rock and
ultimate source of joy and inspiration*

*And to the neurodiverse among us,
and those supporting them on their journeys*

Contents

Foreword

Blockchain technology is seeing the fastest pace of adoption of any technology in human history. It is growing at twice the speed of the internet when it had the same number of users back in 1997.

As you have picked up this book, you probably have an interest in this new technological breakthrough. You might be interested in investing in cryptocurrencies or seeing if blockchain could help you solve long-standing business problems. Many of you might not think it will affect you directly, but it is literally going to change everything – from the entire financial system to the predominant global business models.

As a global macro investor, someone who scours the world looking for the best performing asset classes or markets to invest in, it is my job to assess new opportunities that arise and dynamically calculate the chances of success. That led me to bitcoin and then to the entire world of digital assets built on blockchain technology.

My own journey in crypto and blockchain began – as it does with many people – with bitcoin. Back in 2012 I had just witnessed the global financial crisis and the European crisis, advising many of the world's most famous hedge funds how to navigate it. Luckily, I even forecast both crises long before they came to pass, and it had become strikingly clear that our hugely over-leveraged financial system was creaking at the seams. We also learned that no one knew who owned anything anymore, as layers of leverage had been built upon each other, creating a giant house of cards.

It was then I discovered bitcoin and distributed ledger technology, and I saw that it could be the basis for an entirely new financial system. This technology allowed not only for the trusted and proven ownership of financial assets, but had created a system of money that lay outside of the realm of governments, which had discovered the printing presses as their only answer to the debt problem.

At this point, I had only a superficial knowledge of the application of blockchain as it was still nascent, but over time I realised that it was likely to become the cornerstone to all financial market operations – settlement, custody, clearing, ownership and transfer. Essentially all equities, bonds, credit instruments, derivatives, currency, etc, are likely to go onto a blockchain. Then it became clear that decentralised finance (DeFi) was going to disrupt borrowing and lending too.

Even the world's major central banks accepted that the digital world needed digital currency infrastructure. They are building central bank digital currencies to help bring nation states into this ongoing revolution.

However, this is not just the story of the financial system. Non-fungible tokens (NFTs) and social tokens will most likely upend the ownership, storage and transfer of all assets – physical and digital – and bring about the rise of complex adaptive societies (communities) as the predominant business model, where tokens act as both a currency and reward system for those communities, creating profound network effects.

All of this can be thought of as the 'internet of value' and it will all run on blockchain technology.

This is why this book is so important. We all need to educate ourselves about this massive and total disruption of legacy business models. It might seem a little daunting at first, but Conor does a brilliant job at breaking it all down in simple-to-understand chapters that help us learn not only what blockchain does and why it is important but also how it is likely to disrupt all of our futures.

Only the most knowledgeable experts who are also gifted communicators can make complex things sound easy.

Conor Svensson is that rare combination of those two skills. He is deeply experienced and also knows how to make it sound simpler than it is, while still giving an in-depth understanding.

But where Conor really excels is in helping us figure out at a practical level how to be the disruptor or how we might be disrupted, and this book is packed with case studies and clear explanations.

I hope you enjoy *The Blockchain Innovator's Handbook* as much as I did. It is not only an excellent read, but an important one, too.

Raoul Pal, CEO/Co-founder, Real Vision Group, and CEO/Founder, Global Macro Investor

🌐 www.realvision.com

🌐 www.globalmacroinvestor.com

🔲 @RaoulGMI

Introduction

2020 and the Covid-19 pandemic didn't just mark a fundamental shift in the way people work, it also saw widespread adoption of digital assets and blockchain technology. Companies, artists and entrepreneurs started to pioneer new business models and embrace digital assets, finding new ways to capture value and differentiate their offerings.

Ignoring blockchain now is like ignoring the personal computer in the 1980s, the internet in the 1990s, social networks in the 2000s, and smartphones in the 2010s. With an ever-increasing number of products and services being developed with blockchain, we are going to see widespread adoption in the coming years.

It's been over a year since the great reset due to Covid-19 and a new landscape has emerged where:

- Visa, MasterCard and Paypal are all working on blockchain initiatives to service the huge surge in consumer demand for digital assets and address the antiquated payments processing systems.

- Many of the world's largest companies, including Microsoft, Daimler, the DTCC, ING, J.P. Morgan and Vodafone, all have dedicated divisions working with blockchain to provide greater efficiency and transparency to their core businesses.

- The digital assets market has exceeded $2 trillion in value – gold is a $11.6 trillion market.[1]

- There are over 100 blockchain projects with a market capitalisation exceeding $1 billion.

- Tesla, Square, WeWork and *TIME* Magazine started holding digital assets on their balance sheets.

- In the first quarter of 2021, we saw digital artists and collectors trade over $2 billion of blockchain-backed art and collectables as non-fungible tokens (NFTs).[2] These payments were not made using conventional payment rails such as SWIFT, but with digital assets. The figure includes a single image sold by Christies for $69.3 million.

- Over $100 billion is locked into code that lives on decentralised finance (DeFi) platforms.[3]

If you find these figures staggering, you aren't alone. Blockchain and the applications built on top of it have been gaining ever more traction since the emergence of bitcoin in 2009. Gartner has estimated that the business value generated by blockchain will reach $176 billion by 2024, and a staggering $3.1 trillion by 2030.[4]

You are probably a leader within a large organisation with responsibility for an entire business line. You want to know how you can unlock new opportunities with this technology or how it could pose a risk to your existing business. By the end of *The Blockchain Innovator's Handbook* you will:

1. Have identified a number of key opportunities and threats to pay attention to

2. Be armed with the background and vocabulary underpinned by several case studies to ensure you are never caught unaware when asked what your thoughts on blockchain are

3. Understand what it takes to drive transformations with the technology

4. Know how to pitch blockchain to your board or leadership team

Most importantly, you will understand how to approach the implementation of a blockchain opportunity for your organisation, taking you from finding the right opportunity to having a scalable solution in place.

My journey with blockchain began in 2016, although initially I was somewhat sceptical about the promise of the technology. Once I started digging beneath the surface and learning about one of the key blockchain platforms – Ethereum – I became captivated and went down the blockchain rabbit hole full time.

The Ethereum blockchain is the second most influential blockchain platform after Bitcoin.[5] Unlike bitcoin, which is considered digital gold, Ethereum can be thought of as a decentralised computer running on top of the internet. Most of the innovations we see currently with blockchain and cryptocurrency have stemmed from one of these two platforms. We'll be diving deeper into these in subsequent chapters.

What sucked me into Ethereum was that it reminded me of my experience in the late 1990s with Linux. Linux was a free computer operating system that displaced proprietary Unix operating systems from the likes of IBM, Hewlett-Packard and Sun Microsystems, and ultimately became responsible for powering the majority of the internet's infrastructure and Android smartphones.

Like Linux, I could see that Ethereum was more than just a technology, it was a movement, and I wanted to be a part of it. There was a lot of talk about the transformative potential of blockchain technology for business, but there was no easy way to get the enterprise software platform of choice – the Java virtual machine (JVM) – to talk to Ethereum.

I had spent more than the first decade of my career working on the Java platform at some of the world's largest financial institutions, so it felt like a natural problem to address. This culminated in me authoring the Web3j blockchain software library, which has since been downloaded over 1 million times and is used by companies such as Samsung, Opera and UBS in their blockchain offerings.

The first iteration of Web3j was released in September 2016. Two months later J.P. Morgan announced its Quorum blockchain technology (now ConsenSys Quorum), which was a pivotal moment for me – here was one of the world's most significant financial institutions demonstrating a keen interest in blockchain. I made some contributions to the project, and in the following months founded Web3 Labs, to support the ongoing development of Web3j and work with organisations wishing to harness the potential of blockchain technology. We have been fortunate in the years since to work with leading enterprises such as J.P. Morgan and Microsoft, alongside blockchain technology companies such as ConsenSys and R3, some of which I expand upon in this book.

I've also supported the development of blockchain standards through my involvement over the years with a number of leading industry organisations.

At the Enterprise Ethereum Alliance, for a number of years I chaired the Technical Specification Working Group, which was responsible for delivering the world's first Enterprise Ethereum specifications. More recently I moved on to serve on the Baseline Protocol's Technical Steering Committee and as vice-chair of the InterWork Framework Working Group at the Global Blockchain Business Council.

My experience of working with leading enterprises and blockchain technology companies, developing widely used software and contributing to industry standards over the years brings a sound foundation upon which I build here.

Blockchain is now well positioned to start having the impact that its proponents have been highlighting for years. The changes to ways of working that businesses have had to embrace as a result of Covid-19 have opened people's eyes as to how quickly change can be embraced and the opportunity it provides for businesses to evolve and enter new markets. This, coupled with the funds that have flown into the sector, and adoption by many of the world's leading businesses and consumers, ensures that belief in the technology is now real and it is already in the mainstream.

The intent of this book is not to provide a treatise that should be studied, but a pragmatic guide to how block-chain can best serve your needs. It is split into three parts.

In Part One, I unpack why blockchain requires you to reimagine what's possible. After all, it's a revolution not an evolution.

In Part Two, I discuss how you can embrace blockchain to find new opportunities for your business.

Finally, in Part Three I show how you can keep the momentum going and are able to take action based on the advice provided.

In the back of the book, you can find a detailed glossary and a number of resources that you will find useful to go deeper into any of the topics discussed here.

Collectively, this will ensure you can be confident you have the right plan of action to innovate with blockchain technology. This will empower you to focus on the areas that will bring the greatest long-term value for your business and ensure that it is you who can become the disrupter, rather than being disrupted.

PART ONE

THIS TIME IT'S DIFFERENT

Many disruptive technologies promise how they will challenge the status quo, bringing new efficiencies to business and changing the world in the process.

Blockchain is one such technology. However, like highly disruptive technologies such as the internet before it, its reach is significant with implications for society as a whole.

In this part I'll be discussing both what it is and how it's going to impact the world.

1

The Machine You
Cannot Shut Down

To appreciate what's possible with blockchain, we need to lay some foundations. I'm going to start by discussing why this technology is so significant and how it relates to the World Wide Web.

I'm also going to contrast it with another disruptive technology, Apple's App Store, before covering some of the fundamental concepts behind the technology and why it's so exciting.

The unstoppable machine

James Cameron's iconic film *Terminator* depicted a future where machines had risen to be in conflict with the human race. Although the overall premise of the story is familiar to many, the roots of the artificial intelligence known as Skynet that rose up to challenge the human race is less so.

Skynet was a computer network created by the US military, intended to ward off attacks by rogue actors and nations. It used cutting-edge artificial intelligence (AI) technology that ultimately became self-aware, developing its own stream of consciousness. This was a step too far for the creators of Skynet and a cause of great concern. In response the military attempted to shut down Skynet, which resulted in Skynet perceiving its creators as a threat, leading ultimately to a catastrophic war between the human race and machines that was played out in *Terminator* and its many sequels.

You are probably wondering what the tale of this dystopian future has to do with blockchain; you're not here to think about ways in which technology could spell the end of humankind. But there's something very powerful in this story – the notion of an unstoppable machine.

System outages affect everyone, and regardless of how sophisticated technology becomes, you find yourself still being affected on a daily basis by them. It could be something as trivial as a website being down, or a payment portal not working when trying to book a holiday, through to system outages that directly affect your business' bottom line – software tracking real-time profit and loss, inventory management, availability of customer or supplier portals, crucial databases going offline, you get the idea.

These problems resurface time and time again. Imagine for a moment if you had the opposite problem, a machine you couldn't shut down? Imagine how much efficiency you would gain from having a technology driving your business that doesn't just fall over due to an operator error, or data centres going down, which you can rely on being globally available 24/7 to meet the ever-increasing demands of your customers?

If I told you this technology already exists and is gaining widespread adoption, you'd want to learn more right? Fortunately for you, it does already exist in the form of decentralised technologies such as blockchain, powering massively distributed and decentralised computer networks that are unstoppable.

The three World Wide Webs

How is this different from the internet, you may ask? The internet provides connectivity between computers across the world, democratising access to data. This is achieved with common protocols for accessing and sharing data, the hypertext transfer protocol (HTTP) emerging as the dominant one in the 1990s to drive the World Wide Web alongside web browsers. This was Web 1.0.

In the 2000s we saw the emergence of social networks such as Facebook and Twitter, and website indexing services like Google where companies started to add their own layer of value to Web 1.0. Thus emerged Web 2.0, also known as the social web.

However, this centralisation of services on Web 2.0 is less optimal for users. Many of the providers of these services use proprietary technology, and have found ways to monetise their users' data for their own commercial benefit. Additionally, these platforms are still vulnerable to internal outages that can bring down their entire site.[6] They also can exert undue levels of influence on the success or failure of services that run on top of them. For instance, what if you have a highly successful app on Google Play or Apple's App Store that is taken down in error? Or an online business that runs on Amazon's Web Services platform, which suffers an outage and brings your business down in the process?

The next generation of decentralised protocols, known as Web 3.0, address many of these issues. Computation, data storage and data retrieval move to decentralised networks of computers, rather than individual services hosted by companies or service providers that are subject to failure. This allows for the creation of a new generation of companies and services that offer greater efficiency and availability, along with higher degrees of transparency and more equitable access, benefiting all.

	Web 1.0	Web 2.0	Web 3.0
Name	The static web	The social web	The semantic web, the spatial web
Era	1991–2004	1999 onwards	2009 onwards
Key features	Static web pages hosted by internet service providers (ISPs)	Centralised services providing rich dynamic web applications, social media, blogging, podcasting	Decentralisation, open, trustless and permissionless networks. Also encompasses AI, Internet of Things (IoT), 5 G and augmented reality
Notable companies and technologies	AltaVista, Yahoo, Netscape, GeoCities	Google, Facebook, Twitter	Bitcoin, Ethereum, The Interplanetary Filesystem (IPFS)

2008 – a tale of two technologies

The summer of 2008 marked the emergence of two world-changing technologies, both of which have left their mark. However, the true impact of one of them is only just starting to become clear.

On 10 July 2008 Apple launched the first version of its App Store. The App Store was a portal for anyone with an iPhone, launched one year previously, to download and install applications on it. This created an incredible opportunity for Apple, app developers and consumers. Apple took a 30% fee on all transactions, developers were able to innovate and create new experiences for users, and users had a platform where they could easily obtain apps and games optimised for the iPhone.

The App Store has been a hugely successful platform for Apple, with revenues reaching $64 billion in 2020.[7]

Just over one month after the original App Store launch, another big innovation emerged. On 18 August 2008, an anonymous developer[8] using the pseudonym Satoshi Nakamoto released a white paper for a new type of digital currency. Named bitcoin, this digital currency addressed the issue of its predecessors whereby one could transact with another over the internet without requiring an intermediary.

The creation of the bitcoin white paper[9] and the subsequent launch of the Bitcoin network paved the way for other technologies. Bitcoin was a decentralised peer-to-peer (P2P) network of the type popularised by the Napster music-sharing application back in 1999.

P2P networks provided an alternative approach to the dominant client–server architectures of the time where access to resources such as processing power or storage was coordinated by centralised servers. With P2P, resources are distributed among the network participants or peers equally without any centralisation.

In addition to P2P, there was a new type of technology at the heart of the bitcoin protocol called a blockchain, which was the data structure used to store details of all the transactions taking place on the network.

As ground-breaking as it was, one of the perceived limitations of bitcoin is that it was designed to be a digital currency, and limited to supporting use cases around payments. In 2013, Vitalik Buterin, aged only nineteen, published a white paper proposing a new type of blockchain network, one that could support general purpose computation.[10,11] This network was known as Ethereum, and was another crucial evolution in decentralised technology.

This first-generation blockchain foundation laid by Bitcoin and subsequently improved upon in its second generation by Ethereum have been two of the major driving forces behind the emergence of blockchain during the past decade. The flexibility offered by Ethereum, with its support for general purpose computation, caught the attention of people and organisations around the world. They recognised the opportunity it provided for streamlining many of their increasingly complex business processes across a web of companies and intermediaries spread globally.

In the time that blockchain has slowly ascended from being a niche technology on the fringes of society to obtaining mainstream acceptance, Apple's App Store established itself as a platform for companies to reach over half a billion people around the world each week,[12] with the ability to make or break businesses.

Why have we not yet seen blockchain establish itself as a crucial piece of plumbing in our society, like the App Store, which the majority of the developed world engages with almost constantly to the point of being considered an addiction?[13]

Blockchain is, of course, a fundamentally different innovation, one that was not originally created with commercial intent to exploit and grow a product ecosystem ultimately benefiting a commercial entity and shareholders. It is a new foundational layer that rewrites the rules of how companies can exist and operate on the internet.

Disruptive innovations don't just offer incremental improvements to the status quo, they shift the landscape rendering previous innovations obsolete. When the first transcontinental railroads were laid in the United States in the 1860s, it facilitated trade between the previously isolated West Coast and the East Coast. This provided a huge growth opportunity for businesses. This innovation changed what was possible. Instead of it taking months to travel from one side of the US to the other by a horse-drawn cart, it was now possible in a week, and without the same restrictions on the volumes of goods that could be transported. By 1880, about $50 million of freight was being moved by railroad.[14]

The railroad allowed new classes of business to be established by entrepreneurs and innovators who were savvy enough to challenge the status quo and exploit the opportunities it provided in logistics. It also allowed new communities to be built, servicing the stops along the railroad as well as turning California from an isolated location into a major economic and political force.

Much like how the intercontinental railroad created the foundations for linking communities and businesses, the past decade or so has seen these decentralised foundations being laid. An ever-increasing number of individuals and companies are finding ways to create new types of efficiency and value for those who choose to embrace these decentralised networks.

We are now at the point where billion-dollar companies and blockchain protocols are being created to service the demand that has emerged. This is in part because many of the technical and geographical limitations of the technology have been addressed. Just as importantly, we're starting to see regulatory frameworks emerge in many of the world's most powerful nations, including the UK, Switzerland, Germany, Singapore and the United States, that strengthen blockchain's foundations.

Unlike the App Store, which is primarily a B2C (business-to-consumer) platform that has been able to proliferate rapidly thanks to widespread internet connectivity, blockchain is just getting started. It is providing a new class of opportunities, not just for both B2C and business-to-business (B2B), but also wider impactful initiatives that will leave no sector untouched – financial, telecoms, supply chain, gaming, property, healthcare, government and social.

The 2010s may have been the decade of the App Store, but the 2020s will be the decade of blockchain.

Blockchain and distributed ledger technology

So far, we have discussed the emergence of the Bitcoin and Ethereum networks and where the idea of a blockchain came from, but we haven't gone into any detail of what a blockchain is, and how this ties in with other concepts that are used with it interchangeably, such as distributed ledger technology (DLT).

There are plenty of resources you can read to get a detailed overview of how blockchains work (see the Resources section at the end of the book). My intent here is to provide enough detail to understand the fundamentals so we can build upon them in subsequent chapters.

BLOCKCHAIN MYTH: Dispelling commonly held beliefs about blockchain

In this first part of the book as I discuss some of the core concepts and innovations related to blockchain, I've inserted a number of sections like this to help dispel common myths or confusion about blockchain.

The first of these to address is that blockchains and distributed ledgers are not the same thing. A blockchain is a category of distributed ledger technology, which I explain in more detail below.

Distributed ledger technology

Strictly speaking, blockchain is a type of DLT, which is an electronic ledger of transactions that is stored in a distributed format across multiple computers.

In a standard ledger, like the sort used in financial bookkeeping, there are entries on each line for transactions that take place. In our example below, we have a simple ledger for a company named Cyber Research Systems, which contains a number of debit and credit transactions.

By tallying up the transactions on the ledger, you can ascertain the ownership of an asset (in this case money) by an individual at a point in time.

Entry#	Date	Description	Debit	Credit	Balance
0	6th July 2021	Opening Balance	–	–	1,000,000
1	24th July 2021	Services for E. Corp Inv.#197	–	750,000	1,750,000
2	25th July 2021	Weyland Corp Inv.#2871	250,000	–	1,500,000
3	27th July 2021	Meta Corp Inv.#531	500,000	–	1,000,000
...	...	...	...	...	...
			...	...	...
1023	21st March 2023	Service for Epiphyte Corp Inv.#978	...	2,949,000	22,949,000

A financial ledger showing the balance at a point in time

The other organisations which our company is sending payments to or receiving payments from will have their own transaction ledgers with their own records of these transactions. This is the widely used double-entry book-keeping accounting approach.

Instead of having this information stored in a single file such as a spreadsheet on a computer for each organisation, a distributed ledger consists of multiple identical copies of this ledger file distributed to all computers on a network. This ledger tracks the ownership of assets across all companies or individuals across the network. This is achieved by following a common set of rules for the network, known as its protocol.

When an update is made to a copy of the ledger by someone interacting directly with one of the computers on the network, that computer must first validate the update, then propose the update to the other participants on the network. Again, this is achieved by following the network's protocol. When this update is processed by the other participants they must reach agreement (referred to as consensus) on whether to accept this update.

Given the distributed nature of these computers, they each process the update independently, based on their own view of the world, then they communicate their updated state of the ledger. These computers all abide by the same rules encoded in the software they run, so these updates, although applied individually, will be the same across the network, resulting in a consensus of the ledger.

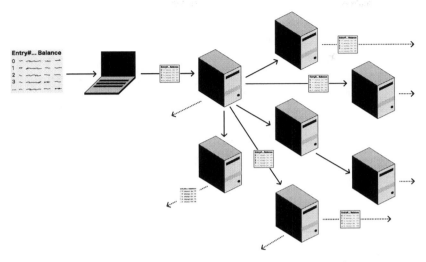

A digital ledger being distributed across a network

This underlying protocol, dictating how a common state is reached via consensus across a distributed network of computers, is the hallmark of a distributed ledger technology such as the Bitcoin or Ethereum networks.

Blockchain

A blockchain is a type of data structure that is used to store details of the transactions that take place on a distributed ledger. A blockchain can be thought of as a master record or log of transactions that have taken place on a distributed ledger. It is visible to all participants, and is representative of not just one company's transactions, but those of all participants on the network.

Suppose you are working with a tabular ledger in book form and you wish to record a new transaction. You read down the table and record the new transaction at the bottom of the table. The previous transaction is recorded one line above where you are. Details of these transactions are considered immutable, as you do not delete existing transactions when you add new ones.

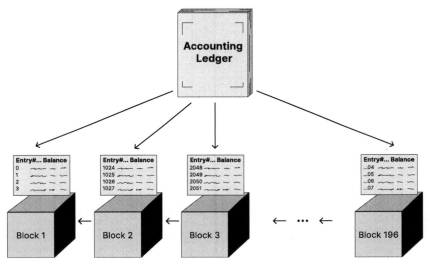

Pages from a ledger grouping blocks of transactions

When you fill up a page of the ledger, you turn it and start adding new transactions on a fresh page. You can think of each page as holding a group or block of transactions. There is a natural ordering to these pages as they come one after another, linked together by the binding or held together in a chain.

This immutable chain of blocks, which hold groups of transactions from all participants, is what defines a blockchain.

This blockchain acts as the single source of truth for all participants on the network.

In understanding the fundamentals of blockchain and DLTs, you are armed with foundations you need to start understanding this fascinating space in more detail.

BLOCKCHAIN MYTH: Blockchain is slow

The decentralised nature of blockchain networks does limit the throughput they can achieve compared with smaller, centralised systems. Historically, the greater the level of decentralisation people wished to achieve with blockchain networks, the more throughput would suffer. However, with the advent of private-permissioned blockchain platforms and the emergence of third-generation blockchain platforms (see Chapter 2), some of which are dedicated to scaling the Bitcoin and Ethereum networks, this is increasingly becoming less of a consideration.

Summary

Since its emergence in the 1990s, the World Wide Web has gone through three major iterations:

- Web 1.0: the static web

- Web 2.0: the social web

- Web 3.0: the semantic or spatial web

Bitcoin and the App Store both emerged in the summer of 2018 and, while having undertaken very different trajectories, are both highly influential innovations.

At the heart of the Bitcoin and Ethereum networks is a type of distributed ledger technology, a blockchain. A blockchain groups transactions into blocks and distributes them across computers on a decentralised network.

2

The Safest Place For Your Data Is Everywhere

In this chapter, we will further explore why decentralised technology provides such a powerful approach to data storage. We will also expand further on some of the core concepts of blockchain and DLT technology that provide the common abstractions that are familiar to many users.

Decentralised is safer

Everyone has important data they want to protect. In the real world most people find time to create a last will and testament, which is an expression of whom they wish to pass their assets on to after they die. This document is often accompanied via supplementary documents that provide details of their core assets, such as bank accounts, title deeds, investments and life insurance policies. This ensures that when they die, their beneficiaries can obtain those assets in a relatively straightforward manner.

The information contained within those documents is sensitive. If it ended up in the wrong hands it could potentially be used for identity fraud and other malicious actions. Hence it needs to be stored in a secure manner. It could also be catastrophic for some if lost, as anyone inheriting assets who isn't a blood relative could have a hard time proving they were allocated certain assets.

For this reason, it's important that access to these documents is controlled and that multiple copies are created and distributed in a secure manner. With physical documents, this means that multiple copies often end up in bank safety deposit boxes, different banks, storage facilities, or residing with solicitors or lawyers. The executor of the estate needs to be able to access these documents, to ensure that assets are distributed to the right people in accordance with the will.

The creator of the will may, depending on the value of their assets and the perceived stability of the region where they reside, wish to distribute their assets across a number of geographic locations, or even subdivide the legal documents, so no single location has all of the crucial information. The documents could be spread among different banks within their city, further afield in other regions, or even countries. The more this important information is distributed, the less likely it is to be lost, providing the owner has a way to recall which parts are in which locations.

Such distribution also ensures that if someone were to access one of the locations, they wouldn't be able to piece together a full picture of that person's assets or wishes, providing further safety for the individual and those who stand to benefit from their wishes when they die.

It's no different when we jump into the digital world. From the above, hopefully it's clear that the safest way to store your data is everywhere – the more copies you have, in the more physical locations, the less likely it is ever to be lost. Of course, privacy and access restraints need to be in place, to ensure only the right persons can piece it back together, but the more duplication there is the safer it is. This is the notion at the heart of decentralised technologies like blockchain.

In distributing copies of the blockchain transaction ledger across tens of thousands of computers spread around the world, blockchain networks provide a level of data availability and redundancy that is unparalleled in centralised systems.

BLOCKCHAIN MYTH: Blockchain creates needless duplication of data

The duplication of data in blockchains is required to fulfil the data availability guarantees of the system. If this data is not duplicated to all nodes, the chance of data loss increases. In distributed systems, there is always a trade-off in the availability and consistency of data, and resiliency to communication breakdowns. This is such a well-known problem that a theorem in computer science, the CAP theorem, was created for it. It implies that in the presence of a failure or partition in a computer network, one has to choose between consistency and availability of data: you cannot have both.[15]

Sounds great, but at what cost?

Historically, two of the main trade-offs associated with this approach used by blockchains are speed and privacy. Consensus or agreement needs to be reached by the majority of network participants before new transactions can happen, and the contents of the underlying transaction ledger are visible to all participants.

In the real world if you had a document that was split between multiple physical secure locations, it would be time-consuming and require physical authentication to access the document and piece it back together. Hence if it doesn't contain any sensitive information, you may be prepared to compromise on this level of security and store it in a folder by your desk where you can quickly refer to it.

The scaling and privacy limitations are issues that are being addressed with rapidly evolving scaling technologies and new approaches to privacy that make them of far less concern than they were when these networks were first launched. I won't go into detail here, but if you're curious I encourage you to take a look at zero-knowledge proofs, which are defined in the glossary.

Cryptocurrencies

Given these blockchain networks run on the internet, surely anyone can access them? And, yes, just like a website, anyone with an internet connection can access them. But unlike websites, blockchain networks have significant value associated with them.

The Bitcoin network provides a digital store of value in the form of the bitcoin currency, and Ethereum provides a platform for computation. There must be a cost to running these networks, and you need to protect them from malicious agents, so how is this achieved? The answer lies in the consensus mechanism of the network and the real-world cost required to have a say in how the consensus is reached.

Cryptocurrencies are a store of value that is coupled to a blockchain network. Anyone who wishes to use a network must pay a fee, typically in its native cryptocurrency. In the case of the Bitcoin network, just like with a credit card payment, a proportion of the bitcoin sent via the network to someone else is taken as a fee. In the case of Ethereum, someone must pay using ether, the network's native cryptocurrency to execute computer code on the network.[16]

The types of action performed depend on the functionality offered by a particular blockchain and may vary from simply sending cryptocurrencies from one wallet to another, to complex, decentralised application interactions.

The fees associated with the usage of blockchains often go back into the network and are distributed as rewards to the computers that are collectively running the network.[17] The computers bundle transactions together in blocks, as outlined in the previous chapter, proposing new blocks for the blockchain. These computers are called miners because they create new blocks for the network and help to secure it. The mechanisms by which these blocks are proposed are dictated by the consensus mechanism of the network.

The combination of transaction fees and block creation work as an incentive mechanism for individuals and companies to run computers that contribute to the overall health and availability of networks.

BLOCKCHAIN MYTH: Blockchain consumes a lot of energy

The type of consensus mechanism used in a blockchain network dictates how agreement is reached among participants. There are a number of different mechanisms, the most well-known being proof of work (PoW) and proof of stake (PoS). These mechanisms erect barriers to entry for participation in the network that have a real-world cost. In the case of PoW it is computational power which uses a lot of electricity, and in the case of PoS it is cryptocurrencies that require capital.

The PoW consensus used by the Bitcoin and Ethereum networks does use a large amount of electricity (although Ethereum is transitioning off it in favour of PoS in 2022). However, they are the exception rather than the norm. The third-generation platforms typically use a version of PoS; and private-permissioned blockchains, which we discuss later, support a number of types of consensus.

Although cryptocurrencies are coupled to the blockchain network they support, interest has grown in them to the extent that they are considered an asset class in their own right, collectively referred to as the digital asset market. Bitcoin's steady growth in value is reflected in its reaching a market capitalisation of over $1 trillion in 2021, while Ethereum's ether cryptocurrency reached over $400 billion market capitalisation. The overall digital asset market capitalisation exceeds $2 trillion.[18]

An entirely new field of research known as token economics has also emerged, driven by this market interest in crypto-currencies, where researchers analyse the economic factors and mechanisms that are used to create value across these digital asset and blockchain ecosystems.

Nice wallet, where did you get that?

Digital assets such as cryptocurrencies have to be stored somewhere and, just like physical cash, they are stored in wallets. Cryptocurrency wallets need to be digital for obvious reasons, but really all they are is a cryptographic key that has a balance of cryptocurrency associated with it. A cryptographic key is an incredibly large number that is used to perform cryptographic operations such as authen-tication and encryption.

These cryptographic keys can be dressed up in multiple ways. They can reside on devices such as your phone, they can be on physical hardware wallets, or even written down on paper that can be stored in a similar way to a last will and testament. Many cryptocurrency exchanges also manage them on behalf of their customers to simplify the user experience (although your funds are not protected if the exchange is hacked).

Cryptographic keys are not an unfamiliar type of technology. The entire security model of the internet known as transport-layer security (TLS), which allows you to safely provide your credit card details on a website (you notice that lock icon in your browser on those sites, right?) to purchase goods, uses exactly the same type of cryptographic concepts, just for a slightly different use case.

As there is a cryptocurrency balance associated with these wallets or keys, they are referred to as accounts, as they are ultimately what transactions on a blockchain are associated with. There are abstractions that can be used to associate them with an entity such as a person or company, but when you strip away the abstractions that is what is left. For the purpose of understanding how they fit into blockchain it's important you remember, blockchain wallets just store regular cryptographic keys. The actual digital assets associated with a wallet do not reside in the wallet itself, the ownership is tracked on the underlying blockchain. The wallet simply holds the cryptographic keys that can be used to prove ownership of the asset and allow the current owner to transfer those assets to another digital wallet.

BLOCKCHAIN MYTH: The transition to quantum will break the security underpinning cryptocurrencies

Quantum computing has the potential to break current cryptographic keys underpinning blockchain networks. If this were to happen it wouldn't affect only blockchain and cryptocurrencies, but the entire security model of the internet, including the above-mentioned TLS that is used for processing credit card details. So, as quantum technology becomes closer to realisation, the internet as well as cryptocurrency and blockchain networks will need to adopt quantum-resistant cryptography practices.

Smart contracts

We've discussed the incentive mechanisms for blockchain networks – cryptocurrency and how you store it in wallets – but what can you actually do with them? The Bitcoin network allows people to send bitcoin to each other. You saw this is possible with Ethereum too. However, we also mentioned that Ethereum is a globally distributed computer network – how does that work and what does it mean? The answer lies in smart contracts.

A smart contract is computer code that you write and can run on top of a blockchain network. Being able to execute arbitrary computer code across massively decentralised distributed computers is one of the key innovations powering the blockchain ecosystem, creating entirely new types of business opportunities and efficiencies.

What this means is that business logic to support an activity can be coded and deployed to a blockchain network as smart contracts. Those entities that interact with the deployed smart contracts are all governed by the same rules defined in the business logic, which is ultimately controlled by the blockchain and itself an entity that none of them can exert undue control over. This results in a fairer, more efficient and transparent mechanism by which people and companies can do business with one another. Contrast this with traditional computer networks, where trusted intermediaries coordinate activity between participants. In blockchain networks you remove the need for these intermediaries – they are disintermediated by these smart contracts. This has the effect of greater transparency and security across the network, while also reducing costs and fees for participants as they no longer need to go through an intermediary.

This foundational layer creates all sorts of new opportunities for innovation, which we'll be digging into in subsequent chapters.

Decentralised storage

Although blockchains and distributed ledgers focus on dealing with transactions that support cryptocurrencies and the execution of code as smart contracts, another crucial component of the decentralised ecosystem is decentralised storage.

Be it a scan of a physical document, a digital document or an image, we've already discussed the potential benefits that decentralisation can bring to increasing the availability, durability and security of crucial data. Decentralised storage technologies provide the mechanism to achieve this.

On the surface, decentralised storage technologies are not dissimilar to other established storage approaches used on the Web; to the user they provide some sort of gateway or portal to upload a document or files that can later be retrieved using a similar mechanism. The difference with decentralised storage technologies is where the underlying data itself goes.

With conventional storage, the files reside on a computer or dedicated storage devices that are operated by a single company or provider. In the decentralised world a computer network stores the data in chunks, which is duplicated and spread across the thousands of computers making up the network.

As with blockchain networks, users pay for the storage and retrieval of data by users with a cryptocurrency, which compensates those providing the computing power that runs the network for doing so.[19]

This decentralised storage approach was pioneered by the Interplanetary Filesystem project (IPFS).[20] IPFS provides a decentralised storage layer for the internet and it is complemented by the Filecoin project, which provides decentralised storage services for IPFS and a token to incentivise participants.[21]

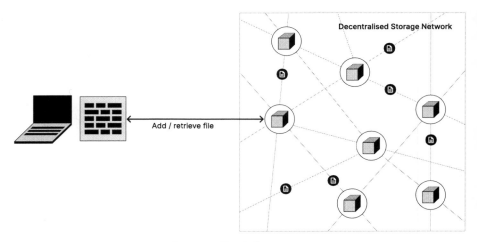

Decentralised file storage

As ground-breaking a development as decentralised storage is, we will focus less on this technology in the pages that follow. Although it is a crucial building block for fully decentralised systems, the paradigms that need to be embraced to understand the opportunity it provides are not as formidable as those associated with blockchain, which I'm keen to ensure you stay focused on as that's the technology that probably presents the greatest opportunity for you.

The next generation

More recently we've seen the emergence of third-generation blockchain platforms. These platforms address some of the perceived limitations of the Bitcoin and Ethereum networks, such as their limited transaction throughput and support for interoperability with other blockchains.

Some of these provide a separate network for scaling that runs alongside the main Ethereum network, such as Polygon and Optimism. Others provide an entirely separate blockchain, such as Polkadot, Cardano and Solana.

As the landscape of third-generation blockchain platforms is rapidly evolving, I don't discuss them in detail here, but I do list the major protocols in the Resources section of the book.

	1st generation	2nd generation	3rd generation
Start of era	2008	2013	2017
Key features	Blockchain, cryptocurrencies	Smart contracts and general purpose computation	Scaling, interoperability
Protocols	Bitcoin	Ethereum	Cardano, Polkadot, Avalanche, Solana, Polygon, Optimism

Public versus private networks

The Bitcoin, Ethereum and third-generation networks are globally available, as they run out in the wild on top of the internet. Anyone can access these networks provided they have connectivity to the internet.

Due to their widely accessible, public nature they are referred to as public blockchain networks. Anyone who accesses them can view details of the transactions that are taking place on them. The details of whom transactions are between can be obfuscated, with the payload encrypted, but the transactions themselves still take place on a globally accessible ledger. Additionally, anyone transacting on these networks needs to hold the native token or cryptocurrency.

Private blockchain networks exist on a private network that is only accessible to a defined group of participants. It is up to the creator of the private network to define how agreement or consensus is reached as public cryptocurrencies do not need to be used to control the network, unlike their public counterparts. They also provide more fine-grained privacy and permissioning controls.

The most popular private blockchain network technologies are ConsenSys' Quorum (formerly from J.P. Morgan), R3's Corda and IBM's Fabric. Quorum's technology is similar to the public Ethereum technology with additional privacy and consensus features, whereas Corda and Fabric are used exclusively for private blockchain network deployments.[22]

BLOCKCHAIN MYTH: Encrypting sensitive data on blockchains creates a honeypot of opportunity for attackers

If sensitive data is simply encrypted and stored on a blockchain it could create a honeypot for attackers. However, when sensitive information is being exchanged between participants on a blockchain, the data exchange is not usually recorded on the blockchain itself, only a proof that some exchange took place or event happened.

This ensures that the sensitive data could never be inferred by a malicious actor, as all that resides on the blockchain is a proof that can only be interpreted by those parties who were privy to the actual data exchange.

A new class of cryptographic proof, called a zero-knowledge proof, has emerged in recent years that allows one party to prove to another party that they know the value of something without having to share any information apart from the fact they know the value. This area is rapidly evolving and is likely to have significant bearing on how privacy and scaling is achieved on public blockchains.

Summary

When we wish to store sensitive data, we create multiple copies of it for redundancy purpose. Provided there are adequate security measures in place to restrict access to it, this approach is safer than having a single copy in one location.

Digital assets such as cryptocurrencies provide a store of value and control for interacting with blockchain networks. They are stored in digital wallets.

Smart contracts allow you to run decentralised applications (DApp) on blockchain networks.

Decentralised storage technologies are another component of the blockchain ecosystem that increase the availability, durability and security of data.

Third-generation blockchain platforms are emerging that address the speed and interoperability concerns levied at public blockchain networks.

Public blockchains:

- Use cryptocurrencies to transact with them
- Transactions are publicly visible; privacy approaches are gradually emerging
- Accessible to anyone via the internet

Private blockchains:

- Control over access and privacy
- Transactions only visible to participants and support private types of transactions
- DIY participant onboarding and network management

3

A Future Tale

So far I have discussed why blockchain is such a powerful force for change. In order to further solidify the ways in which it can affect everyday life, it's helpful to look to the future and highlight ways in which it can become embedded in our lives behind the scenes, supporting everything from virtual reality to electric vehicle charging. In this chapter I unpack what parts of this future could look like.

A day in the life

It's been just over ten years since the global Covid-19 pandemic, and you've woken up in your hotel room in Singapore. You reach for your phone to check for messages.

Your friend Leyla has sent you a message about the virtual reality gig you attended last night. Using your VR headset, you were there up close with the Rolling Stones as they performed *Jumping' Jack Flash* for the very last time. You spent that little bit extra to get an exclusive ticket, which lives permanently in your digital wallet.

This ticket is not only proof that you attended this milestone event, but is also an exclusive collectable that enables the holder to replay that event and bring their friends with them whenever they want. Down the line, if you decide you'd like someone else to relive that experience you can sell it on via a digital collectables marketplace. Regardless of how much you sell it for, a set percentage of the sale price is split between the band and the event organisers, and the rest is yours after the marketplace has taken its fee.

Most of the possessions you have purchased lately sit in your digital wallet. It's so much easier having everything in one place rather than spread across a series of emails, websites and platforms, as used to be the case a decade ago.

You decide to listen to some music to get yourself ready for the day ahead; you see that your favourite rapper, Nas, has released a new album that you want to check out. As you start listening, details of this play are being recorded and you can see how much he is being paid as you listen to his latest album. Although you don't think it's his best work, you keep it playing to maximise the royalties he receives.

You need to check out of your hotel today, and you're struck by how much easier it is now then it used to be. You just touch your smart watch on a reader when you leave the room to lock the door, then again when you leave the hotel. Your smart watch is connected to your digital wallet, which contains your digital identity. You used your digital identity to enter into an agreement with the hotel for the booking, and the funds for the trip were held in escrow via a smart contract until you checked out, when they were automatically released to the hotel at the end of your stay.

Outside the hotel a fleet of self-driving taxis is plugged into chargers, waiting to take guests where they need to go. You get into one, which initiates a disconnection from the charging point. The charging point notifies the taxi of how much the charging session cost and takes payment for the session automatically. The charging cable is then released and the taxi heads off to the airport.

En route the taxi automatically pays a series of tolls for travelling on the express highway to the airport; again, these are made using micropayments, this time communicating over a 5G mobile network to the agency responsible for maintaining the highways in Singapore.

Once you reach the airport, you are notified of the total cost of the journey, including tolls, which you approve. Unlike ten years previously, there is no payment provider here – payment goes out of your digital wallet directly to the taxi operator.

You already have your plane ticket sitting in your digital wallet, so you head straight to security and passport control, where you make use of your digital identity again.

Your digital identity is also linked to your digital passport – long gone are the days of having to show an actual passport. Now, all you have to do is scan a QR code at passport control using your digital wallet and approve sending a message to prove who you are. The facial recognition software on your phone's camera is used to prove that the person scanning the code is the real person associated with that identity. You're then free to head into the departure lounge.

You grab a coffee, which tastes surprisingly good for an airport coffee. There's a QR code on the cup that you scan with your phone. This takes you to a site where you can see that the beans came from the district of Lintong Nihuta, to the south-west of Lake Toba on the Indonesian island of Sumatra, with pictures of the family who harvested them. From there the beans travelled to Singapore, where they were roasted only two weeks ago before being distributed to the coffee shop you're at now. Sure, it's only a cup of coffee but when it tastes this good, it's great to know what made it the way it is.

While sitting around, you take a quick look at your asset portfolio. You have holdings in various digital assets that are all generating incomes of 5–15% annually, regardless of how small an amount you have of them. Some of these are riskier than others, but they balance out. You also hold digital dollars, euros and pounds, which are all generating yields at the lower end of this range, but way better than what your bank used to give you.

Some income has come through from the rental property you own in London with your sister. You have a smart contract that receives the rent each month and automatically splits the revenue between you both, and it shows up in your digital wallet. You take some of the income and invest it in a blockchain start-up that is providing provenance of minerals on Mars – the first manned flight is planned a few years from now.

Your airline sends you a message about how you'd like to offset the carbon emissions from your flight. To speed up the transition to net-zero emissions in the airline industry, paying for offsets is a mandatory component of all ticket sales. These offsets are created by a number of different clean energy projects with their origin tracked on a block-chain. You select a wind power project in Madhya Pradesh, India that will ultimately offset 1.23 million tonnes of carbon dioxide equivalent (tCO_2e) over seven years. In your airline's app, you can see that 4.66 digital tCO_2e tokens have been purchased from this project, assigned to your digital wallet to offset the 4.66 tonnes of CO_2 generated by the flight.

You check into social media to get some commentary from the people that inspire with no-BS advice and thoughts. You tip some of them with a micro-transaction as a thank-you for keeping you inspired. It used to be so expensive to do this back when you had to use credit cards – there was a minimum fee of 50 cents for the vendors – whereas now it's nice to be able to send fractions of a cent as easily as you like a post on social media.

You also realise that your travel insurance policy is coming up for renewal. You had to make a few claims in the past year due to missed flights, but prior to that claims were minimal. When you provide your digital ID to other insurers, you're able to easily share your claim records for the past five years and they see that this past year has been different to those prior, so it's not too difficult to find a firm to renew with.

You're going to have a long flight back to London, so rather than risk the choppy internet connectivity you still get on aeroplanes (but hey, at least they don't still try to charge you for it), you head back online to a digital marketplace to purchase some second-hand clothes for your avatar in *Grand Theft Auto 7*. You find some awesome retro Air-Max trainers that were part of a limited digital edition issued by Nike; you can't believe someone is happy to sell them. Your avatar is getting the wardrobe you wish you could have.

You're now feeling all set for your flight; you've got a few hours to yourself where you can immerse yourself in *Grand Theft Auto 7*, before you drift off to sleep and wake up in London, ready to get back to the family.

As challenging as framing the future can be, many of the above scenarios are from a future that is in fact far closer than you think. Companies have already made significant progress in many of the innovations we describe here, in significant part due to the use of blockchain technology.

Summary

Blockchain will have an impact on people's everyday lives in the future. Some of the places it may do this include:

- Provenance of everyday goods such coffee
- Tickets for travel
- Electronic payments
- Investing
- Offsetting emissions
- Virtual reality and gaming
- Payment of music royalties

4

A Timeline Of Innovation

The history of the Bitcoin and Ethereum networks is well documented and we've discussed how blockchain, digital assets such as cryptocurrencies and smart contracts emerged from them. But what are the real innovations and benefits that these technologies have provided to the world? We've suggested where we may be in ten years' time, but how can all of this be possible with the core blockchain technologies that have been outlined thus far?

Why all the fuss about a decentralised world computer such as the Ethereum network? Isn't it just a big, slow computer? Why are digital currencies such a big deal? What can they enable?

To understand the answers to these questions and more, we need to dig further into the major innovations that have come from blockchain technology. It's these opportunities that people and companies have identified that have facilitated the creation of new ecosystems on top of blockchains, creating new billion-dollar industries in the process for brand new types of assets. Yes, some of these are being used for financial speculation. However, they are challenging the status quo, creating new efficiencies never before deemed possible and disrupting long-established creative industries such as the art world.

It all started with smart contracts on the Ethereum network, and something called ERC-20.

Tokenising the world

One of the use cases that was identified early on with blockchain was the ability to create tokens. These tokens can be used to represent anything. A token could represent shares in a company you've created, fractional ownership of a sports season ticket with your friends, or even your own monetary system where you're in control of the monetary policy. The point is that you can pretty much represent anything as a token and easily assign ownership of it.

The great thing about doing it with a blockchain is that the rules governing the ownership are transparent as they exist on the blockchain, and holders of tokens can choose to sell them on should they wish to, all via the blockchain.

They don't need to go through a company or institution's bespoke infrastructure to achieve this. Likewise, access is equitable as it's governed by code that is visible to all network participants. It doesn't matter if you want to have one token or a million, the mechanisms you use are still the same, which provides unprecedented levels of fairness to users.

For example, you could tokenise a luxury residence, enabling buyers of those tokens anywhere in the world to get exposure to an asset class they couldn't normally afford.

This opportunity for creating tokens, or tokenisation of both real-world and digital assets, was recognised in 2015 when the Ethereum network was launched.[23] However, the creation of a token requires an underlying smart contract to manage it, which meant there were many different interpretations of how they could be represented.

This didn't stop people from being able to create tokens per se, but it did make it challenging to understand the tokens that people were creating on the Ethereum network, as they all had their own unique implementations. Fortunately, this didn't last long and a standard was created.

ERC-20

The Ethereum community were influenced by the Internet Engineering Taskforce (IETF), which has been responsible for the creation of a number of the protocols that power the internet. These include TCP/IP and HTTP, which you use to access websites. Ethereum improvement proposals (EIP) to make changes to the Ethereum network can be submitted by anyone, and when those changes relate to smart contracts that run on top of the network, they are named Ethereum requests for comments (ERC), much like the IETF's request for comments (RFCs) that were used to standardise many internet protocols.

In November 2015, Fabian Vogelsteller and Vitalik Buterin proposed ERC-20 which provided a standardised interface for representing tokens in smart contracts on the Ethereum network.[24] It defined common token properties such as their name, symbol and decimal precision for fractionalising them. In addition, it provided common behaviours such as how to transfer tokens from one person to another, and delegate the control of them to someone else. This standard quickly gained support from the Ethereum community.

This meant that if someone wanted to create their own custom token it suddenly became a lot easier – people and companies started creating and sharing reference implementations of smart contracts following the ERC-20 standard. Anyone could take these and deploy to the Ethereum network to support their specific use case.

The birth of the ICO

In order to launch the Ethereum network, the team took a novel approach to raising funds for its development. Rather than make use of established sources of funding such as venture capital, the team raised funds via a type of crowd sale where bitcoin was deposited to a certain wallet address, and in return those investors that deposited bitcoin were given an amount of the cryptocurrency, ether.

Of course, at this time the Ethereum network didn't actually exist, so those early investors were taking a risk that the network might never materialise and they could lose their initial investment. These funds were governed by a non-profit, the Ethereum Foundation, which provided a treasury function overseeing deployment of the funds.

Fortunately for the investors, the network did launch successfully, and they've seen an astronomical return on their initial investment in the years that have followed. This approach to launch the Ethereum network became known as an initial coin offering or ICO where investors invest in a token offered by a prospective project in order to bootstrap a new network or company.[25]

The first great crypto bubble

Given the success of the Ethereum network, coupled with the ERC-20 token standard, a new industry sprang up quickly where companies started raising funds for projects using an ICO. The fundraising was achieved by sending cryptocurrencies to a smart contract on the Ethereum network, and in return investors received tokens that would have some sort of utility once the project was launched. In some cases, this project would run on top of Ethereum, catering for a specific niche such as decentralised insurance or marketplaces. In other cases, it would be to create another base platform to compete with Ethereum (so-called Ethereum killers).

Whatever the objectives, it became a great way for people and projects to raise funds in a crowdsourced way, without the levels of diligence associated with more traditional raising of venture funds. In many cases, all that was required was a white paper describing what was going to be achieved along with a website describing the team.

The industry saw explosive growth during 2017 and 2018 with funds being raised for everything from people's time to sand. During this period, $22 billion[26] was raised by projects, but the market eventually became oversaturated and investors lost appetite for it.

Although it was something of a Wild West, many teams had altruistic goals with what they were setting out to achieve. There were some bad apples in the bunch, too. However, they all touted/offered some kind of token that would be distributed to investors which would provide some underlying value aligned for the long-term benefit of the network and its holders.

The specific value varied from project to project, but broad classes of tokens have emerged.[27]

BLOCKCHAIN MYTH: Cryptocurrencies support criminals

While some criminal organisations use cryptocurrencies for ransom payments and money laundering, the proportion of the cryptocurrency market being used for this compared with fiat currencies such as the US dollar pales in comparison. In 2020 the criminal share of all cryptocurrency activity was only 0.34%, which is approximately $10 billion in transaction volumes, down from 2.1% in 2019. However, the UN estimates that between 2% and 5% of global GDP is connected with money laundering and illicit activity, which equates to between $1.6 trillion and $4 trillion.[28]

Decentralised governance

The decentralised nature of blockchain platforms and applications provides unique approaches to decision-making and governance. By representing the rules underpinning a platform, organisation or application using a smart contract, one can achieve what is described as on-chain governance. Decisions are made by token holders interacting directly with a smart contract and the outcomes are automatically executed as code that exists on the blockchain.

Traditional decision-making, where decisions are made either online or offline, then enacted via some manual steps – be that a software release, or structural change within a company – are considered off-chain, ie they do not take place automatically using code that already exists on the blockchain.

The actual changes to the blockchain network are often implemented in terms of forks. A fork is a modification to the software run by the nodes that make up the network. This can be thought of as a system upgrade spanning the entire network. Two types of fork can take place – soft forks and hard forks.

Soft forks are backward-compatible upgrades to the software. A node that has been updated to the latest version of the software can talk to a node that has been talking to a previous version.

Hard forks are significant changes to the software that are not backward-compatible (referred to more commonly as breaking changes). A node that has been updated to the latest version of the software has a different view of the blockchain underpinning the network compared to one that doesn't. While there are two different versions of the blockchain software running in this instance, it means there are two differing views of the blockchain itself. It has split, or forked, as a result of this. This difference of views is resolved as all nodes are updated, hence fork events usually take place at a well-publicised point in the future to allow all participants to prepare for it in advance.

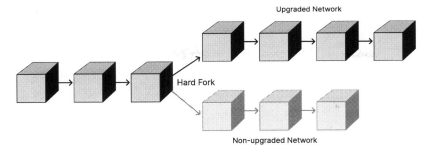

The hard fork of a blockchain network

Both the Bitcoin and Ethereum networks have undertaken hard forks, not only to cater for upgrades, but also because of disagreements in their communities. The end result in the latter case being the creation of additional blockchain networks such as Bitcoin Cash and Ethereum Classic.

BLOCKCHAIN MYTH: Forking blockchains represents a loss of control or intellectual property to business entities

Blockchain forks should be considered analogous to software upgrades. They are necessary to maintain the security and integrity of the system. In a similar manner to how groups such as W3C and IETF define and maintain the key protocols underpinning the internet, those governing blockchain protocols take their responsibility seriously to provide a stable platform for their users. If they didn't their users would simply move to an alternative, more stable platform.

With respect to intellectual property, in the same way that you don't make commercially sensitive information publicly available online, neither should you do this on a publicly available blockchain.

Decentralised autonomous organisations

This notion of fully on-chain governance has enabled people to create decentralised applications that run autonomously on blockchains known as decentralised autonomous organisations or DAOs. Once deployed to a blockchain network, these applications live by the code that was written in the smart contract in which they were created. However, the big difference is that no individual or organisation controls the DAO. It is controlled solely by its token holders.

To become a token holder, you need to send cryptocurrency to the DAO and be allocated tokens, or purchase its tokens via a digital asset exchange. This allows you to vote on decisions that affect what the DAO does, such as how it allocates the funds that have been invested in it by other token holders.

What could possibly go wrong?

You wouldn't be alone in thinking that DAOs sound like quite risky propositions. After all, they exist purely as code running on top of a blockchain and hold funds with real value tied to them.

Back in 2016, a DAO was created on Ethereum and its popularity massively exceeded the expectations of its creators, ending up with over $100 million of the ether cryptocurrency locked up in it just fifteen days after launch. Such a large honeypot on Ethereum didn't go unnoticed and one month later an attacker managed to drain $50 million of ether from it. This ultimately resulted in a hard fork of the Ethereum network in order to rescue those funds. This controversial decision resulted in the creation of the Ethereum Classic[29] network, which consisted of those original Ethereum network participants who weren't willing to adopt the hard fork.

DAOs are still very much an experimental application on blockchains. The lack of emergency control measures built into them means that they can only be as safe as the code that defines them. In addition, their legal classification is a grey area. In some jurisdictions they are being recognised as limited liability entities, but this support is not yet widespread. That said, with the right safety measures behind them, they are a powerful concept that is likely to gain wider adoption as the technology matures.

BLOCKCHAIN MYTH: With a blockchain you lose the control you have with centralised systems to recover from errors

Blockchains relinquish the burden of creating audit trails or proof that activities or events have taken place in applications. This is especially useful when dealing with complex processes spanning multiple internal or external entities. The ability to recover from mistakes or errors should be factored into the design of the decentralised applications that you run on them. While the immutable nature of blockchains does mean that you can't erase erroneous transactions, taking due care in the design of your applications will ensure that you can move on from them.

Classes of tokens

Utility tokens

One of the commonest types of token to emerge is what's known as a utility token. As the name implies, a utility token provides some sort of utility on the network or decentralised application that it is tied to.

You will recall earlier we discussed that ether, the native cryptocurrency of the Ethereum network,[30] is used to pay for the execution of transactions on the network. This is its utility.

Other things that utility tokens can be used for include paying for storage on decentralised file storage networks, compensating those who are running services, or providing value benefiting users of blockchain applications or networks.

Just because it's a utility token doesn't mean that it cannot be used for other means, such as financial speculation. But the primary reason it exists is to provide some utility to users.

Security tokens

Some tokens are treated in a similar manner to conventional securities such as equities, whereby the ownership of the token simply represents ownership of shares in the company. The value of these tokens is then aligned with the perceived value of the company they are associated with.

These types of tokens have been problematic in some jurisdictions due to the regulatory constraints associated with securities issuance. The United States is one such jurisdiction that presents challenges for individuals, which we touch on in Chapter 13.

To cater for institutional demand for ICOs, some companies started undertaking Security Token Offerings or STOs, an evolved type of ICO focusing on more traditional fundraising approaches where investors receive blockchain tokens in return for their investment.

Unlike in an ICO, which generally allows anyone to deposit funds into a public contract in return for tokens, an STO is in effect a private sale to investors who are allocated tokens reflecting their investment.

There are rules that outline how these tokens can be used by investors, such as the vesting periods associated with them and whether they can be used for governance issues such as voting, the mechanics of which can be defined programmatically using smart contracts.

Non-fungible tokens

The tokens that we've covered up until this point can be described as fungible – they are interchangeable, in the same way that one dollar bill is interchangeable for another dollar bill, or if we have shares representing shareholdings in a company, one person's shares are no different to another's, provided they are both the same class.

But what if we want to capture the uniqueness of something digitally – the fact that although the value associated with different dollar bills of the same denomination is the same, the serial numbers used to uniquely identify them are not, or that a piece of art created by one artist is not the same as another. Assets from this perspective are considered unique or non-fungible, and this is another crucial type of token that has emerged.

Like the ERC-20 token standard before it, the discussion started off as an Ethereum improvement proposal, ERC-721, first submitted in September 2017.[31] This was used to establish a standardised way to identify holdings of unique, non-fungible tokens (NFTs). And like its predecessor, it established a foundation upon which an entirely new type of digital asset could be built.

Except this time it wasn't used for raising funds or creating companies, but instead creating digital cats.

CryptoKitties,[32] created by Dapper Labs, were the first big commercial success to come from NFTs. They were so successful that they starting clogging up the Ethereum network upon which they lived. The premise was simple: a smart contract was used to create and breed digital cats with traits of varying rarity that existed as NFTs that people could buy or sell. They were a digital collectable, and demand for them went through the roof.

Other types of digital collectables quickly started to emerge. Tokens were created representing other types of digital items such as avatars, art and objects existing in virtual worlds. Being collectables, marketplaces sprang up to list and sell these tokens. In many cases, royalties were automatically paid to their creators every time they changed hands, providing a new type of ongoing revenue stream for the artists that created them.

Although NFTs followed a very different trajectory to their fungible cousins, the impact they have had is arguably further reaching. We have seen them cross over into the mainstream art world, which started to take note of this billion-dollar market in 2021.

Stablecoins

If you've looked at the price of cryptocurrencies such as bitcoin and ether, you will see it is highly volatile, regularly exposing investors to huge gains and losses. This volatility can be off-putting to those wishing to use these networks for a wide variety of use cases, while normalising this technology. Hence the notion of a new type of digital asset, the stablecoin, was born.

The prices of cryptocurrencies are driven by supply and demand; they are not pegged to any underlying asset. Stablecoins are tokens that exist on blockchain networks whose price is dictated by the underlying fiat currency that they represent. They are not subject to the price fluctuations of cryptocurrencies, and are typically backed by reserves of the underlying asset they represent. As they exist as a token on the underlying blockchain platform, they can be used just like any other token. They can exist in a cryptocurrency wallet and be used anywhere that cryptocurrencies can. This means that they can benefit from the wider financial innovations that are happening on blockchains.

Two of the most widely used stablecoins are Tether's USDT and Circle's USDC, which have over $65 billion in circulation on blockchains.[33]

The new financial infrastructure

The ability to represent fiat currencies such as the US dollar and euro on a blockchain network is one of the mechanisms that is being used to bridge the current financial system to decentralised networks. However, the real change is happening in the new decentralised financial infrastructure, or DeFi, that is being built using smart contracts running on blockchain networks. DeFi requires few of the intermediaries that are commonplace in the world's existing financial infrastructure.

We've already touched on how smart contracts can be used to create investment vehicles based on voting mechanisms such as in DAOs. This autonomy allows them to be used for other financial use cases such as exchanging one type of financial asset for another.

What's so powerful about DeFi is not just the potential to streamline existing infrastructures, but also create a fairer, more transparent and equitable financial system that is accessible to all. The current financial systems mostly benefit the rich, be that individuals, large organisations or banks. Factors such as economies of scale enable them to play by different rules and take advantage of financial products that simply aren't available to the everyday person.

Smart contracts and blockchain networks do not discriminate on the basis of who their users are or where they are located. All they require is an internet connection and some funds to put into this system. Just as the value or geographic location of a payment on a blockchain network has no bearing on its cost, the size of the funds an individual contributes to DeFi applications has no bearing on the return available to them, which provides a more level playing field for finance on a global scale, the likes of which has not been seen before.

Decentralising trading

When someone buys or sells a stock in a company, they usually do this via a broker. The broker uses a stock exchange such as the London Stock Exchange, which facilitates the exchange of money for the stock or vice versa.

Behind the scenes this goes through a clearing house, which is responsible for settling the underlying transaction.

Similar infrastructure has been created for the trading of cryptocurrencies and tokens, whereby exchanges were created solely for the purpose of buying and selling these assets. Unlike a traditional stock exchange, however, the wallets that own the crypto assets being traded exist on the infrastructure of the exchanges, Binance and Coinbase being two of the most prominent. This centralised approach was helpful for making these crypto assets available to a wider group of people, but they are still exposed to the centralisation or counterparty risk that comes with a single entity storing the assets on behalf of its users.

Given that the avoidance of centralisation was one of the problems that blockchain set out to address in the first place, the irony was not lost on the wider community, who wanted to support trading of these assets in a fully decentralised manner. Thus the idea of decentralised exchanges (DEXs) was born.

In a centralised exchange an order book lists what participants are prepared to buy or sell an asset for. Orders sit on the order book until a match between a buyer and seller is found (or is cancelled). This is possible as the exchange has onboarded the participants and knows that they can meet the obligations of either paying for the asset they're buying, or owning the asset they are selling. On these exchanges you have regular market-makers who are participants that provide liquidity to ensure that there is always a market available to buy or sell a specific asset. That is, they make the market in that asset.

In a DEX, smart contracts are used for the exchanging of assets between one party and another, where the smart contract is an automated market-maker (AMM) acting as a broker between the parties.

With an AMM, smart contracts are used to group together or create pools of each type of asset you want to trade, such as a stablecoin and another token or cryptocurrency. Someone can then swap one of the assets supported by that pool for one of the other assets they want. This is called a liquidity pool, as it provides liquidity of the crypto assets it stores to the participants on the exchange. The end-user trading the asset is swapping one type of asset for another, and the exchange is performed via the AMM. Thus the mechanics of a decentralised exchange are some-what different to a traditional centralised exchange.

The image below shows an order book for purchasing ether (ETH) using US dollars (USD). On the left are the prices participants are willing to purchase a quantity of ETH for in USD; on the right are the prices participants are willing to sell it for. The difference in price is called the spread. When there is a match on price, an order executes for the quantity that there is equal demand for.

ETH / USD				
Buyers			**Sellers**	
Qty	Price		Price	Qty
1	**1,999.99**		**2,000.00**	5
8	1,997.86		2,001.96	7
11	1,996.32		2,002.17	25
...	...	Spread = **0.01** USD...		...

A conventional, centralised-exchange order book

In this conventional type of exchange, market-makers are companies or individuals who create buy and sell orders at different price levels for assets in order to provide greater liquidity in the market.

Decentralised exchanges don't have the luxury of knowing who's using them, as there is no onboarding process. Hence the exchange of one crypto asset for another has to take place as a single transaction via a liquidity pool. The ratio of each asset held in a liquidity pool is what determines the underlying trading price, where investors add or remove the assets proportionally to the pool to keep them balanced at a price that is in line with other exchanges, both centralised and decentralised.

This is demonstrated in the image below of a liquidity pool for the stablecoin USDC and ETH. This is established by Alice, the liquidity provider, who deposits USDC and ETH into a smart contract that establishes the liquidity pool.

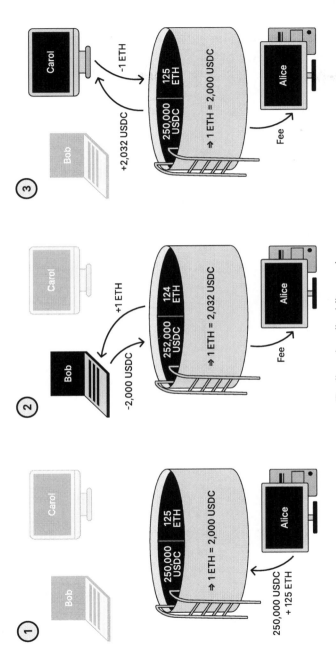

Trading via a liquidity pool

Bob and Carol each then trade with the liquidity pool, exchanging USDC for ETH in Bob's case and ETH for USDC in Carol's. It's important to note here how Bob's transaction affects the ratio of USDC to ETH in his transaction, which subsequently affects the price Carol obtains for her ETH.

As Alice created the pool, the amount of USDC and ETH she owns is dictated by the trading activity in the pool, which she does not control. The potential risk she is exposed to by the ratios in the pool changing significantly is referred to as impermanent loss. To incentivise people like Alice to put their funds into these pools, she earns a fee on every trade that takes place.

One of the leading DEXs is Uniswap, which provides trading assets on Ethereum such as the ether cryptocurrency with other tokens and stablecoins. This approach has since been mirrored across other blockchain networks.

Decentralised lending and yield farming

In much the same vein as the mainstream financial industry continually drove financial innovations during the past fifty years (although many may argue not always beneficially so), entrepreneurs, developers and companies involved with the burgeoning DeFi industry are finding ever more sophisticated ways to generate yield for investors and those seeking a return better than what they get with traditional financial investments.

In addition to DEXs, decentralised lending platforms have emerged that allow individuals to lend cryptocurrencies or tokens they hold to others in return for interest. This incentive can be returned in multiple forms or combinations thereof. It may be in the asset that they are lending or as tokens being created by the platform operator or another cryptocurrency.

On the other side, the borrowers of these assets are providing collateral of equal (and most often greater) value to the asset they are borrowing in return. After all, when you are lending an asset via a public decentralised platform no Know Your Customer (KYC) or equivalent takes place,[34] so the collateral needs to be exchanged up front and is almost always over-collateralised. Why would people borrow these assets then, you may ask? Potential reasons include that they can generate a better yield on the borrowed asset than the underlying asset they own, obtain additional leverage on their assets, or access unrealised gains in a more tax-efficient manner.

These so-called yield farmers go from DeFi platform to DeFi platform to identify the best returns they can generate on their digital assets, creating a web of transactions across smart contracts. There are even more exotic innovations such as flash loans, which facilitate uncollateralised lending of crypto assets,[35] and yield aggregators to help yield farmers maximise their profits. However, we won't go further into these here.

ICO 2.0

The evolution of DeFi has also seen changes to how projects raise funds. In addition to STOs, we've also seen initial exchange offerings (IEOs) where projects raise funds by listing their token on an established cryptocurrency exchange. This is not always optimal as the exchange operator takes an often hefty fee for the service, and exclusivity of the listing is typically required – assuming the exchange is willing to work with them in the first instance. However, the reach to potential investors provided by exchanges is significant, thus frequently making this a worthwhile compromise.

More recently we've also seen the emergence of initial DEX offerings (IDOs) by projects to raise funds. With an IDO, a liquidity pool on a decentralised exchange is created allowing anyone to invest in the token at launch, levelling the playing field for investors. This approach isn't perfect, as there is nothing to stop astute investors from obtaining the majority of the supply before anyone else. Hence platforms that facilitate IDOs have started to emerge that create investment pools known as launchpads. These constrain the amounts of capital that individuals can invest in a single offer, creating a fairer fundraising process for all.

As with other areas of DeFi, the rate of innovation is measured in months rather than years, and these are just the first breed of DeFi applications we're seeing that are contributing to a snowballing $100 billion market.[36]

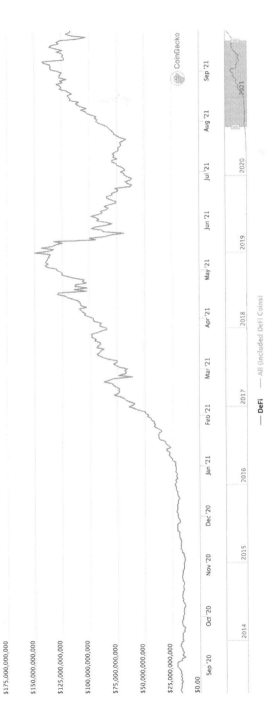

Growth of total value locked (TVL) in DeFi during the past 12 months (Source: www.coingecko.com)[36]

Decentralised identity

Wouldn't it be nice if you didn't have to share personal information every time you signed up to a new online platform or service? The current status quo for signing up for these services seems to be split into one of two buckets:

1. Provide an email address, your name and various combinations of your phone number, date of birth, address, mother's maiden name, first pet's name, city of birth, credit card details, backup email address, passport scans, driving licence scans, bank statements and utility bills... the list goes on.

2. Let Google, Facebook, Twitter, etc share a subset of these private details on your behalf so you don't need to retype them.

Invariably some of these services get hacked and if you're lucky your email is signed up for only a few spam mailing lists.[37] If you're unlucky you get notified that someone has started using your identity – good luck convincing every online service you've ever used that they need to change the information they have about you.

Web-based services are fundamentally broken in their current state. The notion of an individual's or business' identity is recreated again and again with every online service they sign up for. Each service has its own copy of their user's identity; this is not only inefficient for users signing up, but also subject to data quality errors, as inevitably people make mistakes when they fill in form fields.

In addition, you have no visibility of how they're safe-guarding that data.

Or perhaps you're using a social media service to sign up on your behalf – easier, right? But do you really want these services to be learning an ever-increasing amount of information about what you do online that's outside of their ecosystem? The savvy know that when a service is free, you are the product, and this is blazingly obvious when you use these social logins: 'You save me the hassle of providing my details to this online service and you get to know what online services I'm accessing and when in return – deal.'

In the online world, there is no standardised notion of identity, and only a handful of nations support truly electronic identities.[38] We seem destined for a never-ending cycle of giving our information to ever more online services and getting never-ending amounts of spam,[39] or social media platforms learning more and more about our online habits.

Decentralisation provides another way. What if you could register information about yourself on a blockchain, and only provide the minimum data that a third party requires to transact with you?

In a physical shop, a shopkeeper recognises you by your features and you don't need to prove who you are in order to purchase goods, unless you're looking shifty when you bring out that credit card. For the usage of the majority of online services, merchants shouldn't require this either.

This notion of a decentralised identity (DID) has gained significant traction within the online and business communities, with the World Wide Web Consortium (W3C) creating a standard for decentralised identifiers[40] in a similar vein to their already widely used standards that power the internet, such as the HTTP protocol and HTML code.

This is further supported by the work of the Decentralised Identity Foundation and various other industry bodies.

One of the core tenets of DIDs is the notion of verifiable credentials, where the issuer of these credentials is a trusted entity. This credential is tied to a decentralised identifier which is created on a blockchain that has a cryptographic key associated with it. This credential can then be passed by its holder to another party who verifies the claim being made by the credential cryptographically. Hence they can be confident of its authenticity, as there's a layer of trust being provided by the blockchain.

For instance, a government agency could issue you with a verified credential attesting that you're legally allowed to drive a certain class of vehicle. You could then take this credential to a car hire company who cryptographically verifies that the provided verifiable claim matches your decentralised identifier and that it was signed by a known government decentralised identifier.

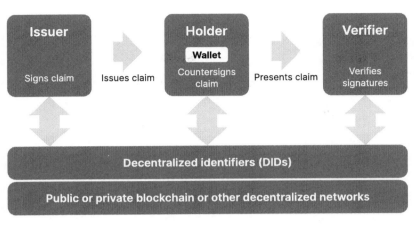

*DIDs enable digitally signed verifiable claims
(Source: Drummond Reed)[41]*

Unlike many of the innovations we have already discussed, those working on DID initiatives are re-architecting what it means to be a digital citizen. This ecosystem, unlike its crypto and DeFi siblings, is less focused on independently spinning up what already exists, but more on working in lockstep with what is already there: finding ways to bridge the gap between blockchain and established platforms that service tens, or even hundreds of millions, of users; and creating a new standard where the rights to privacy and control of data are at the heart of these foundations, rather than an afterthought, as was the case in Web 2.0.

BLOCKCHAIN MYTH: A third party or intermediary can provide the same service as a blockchain

Third parties or intermediaries often sit between organisations, facilitating transactions between them. A clearing house providing settlement of financial transactions is one such example. The issues with intermediaries is that they typically have their own proprietary integration points and little transparency is provided on how their service works internally – you have to trust the intermediary organisation implicitly. A blockchain provides a common protocol for all participants on a network to communicate with each other. The transparent nature of decentralised applications with transactional integrity maintained through cryptographic proofs, ensures that participants have full visibility of the logic encoded within them and can hence explicitly trust the blockchain.

Summary

There have been a number of major innovations that build on top of the foundations of blockchain and cryptocurrencies.

Digital tokens are one key innovation that enables:

- Fundraising of blockchain projects and protocols via ICOs using utility or security tokens

- The creation of digital collectables as NFTs

The smart contracts that power these tokens have also been enablers for other innovations, including:

- Decentralised autonomous organisations

- DeFi, which includes stablecoins, decentralised lending platforms and exchanges

- Verifiable credentials upon which decentralised identity technology is emerging

5

Why 2021 Is The Start
Of The 21st Century

The devastating impact of Covid-19 on communities and economies didn't just force people to change how they worked, it was also the death knell for ways of working for many, some of which practices can be traced back to the second industrial revolution of the nineteenth and early twentieth centuries.

During the mid-twentieth century we saw the emergence of the knowledge economy, whereby workers travelled to offices to use their intellect to facilitate economic and social development. Computers and the internet provided ever greater opportunities to increase the reach of the knowledge economies and started providing greater flexibility for its workers, but change was gradual. Other than the swelling dotcom bubble and concerns about the Y2K bug, the twentieth century transitioned to the twenty-first without much change to the status quo.

This changed in late 2019 with the emergence of Covid-19. By mid-2020 most of the world's countries had responded to the outbreak by closing their borders and sanctioning lockdowns. People who could work remotely did and it forced millions of organisations and individuals to change how they operate on a day-to-day basis. This great reset of people's lives and livelihoods accelerated the transition to digital technologies, forcing changes that were planned five to ten years into the future to take place almost overnight.

There were winners and losers, but the rapid ascension of new ways of working supported by digital technologies marked the end of many long-established working practices. This brings us to where we are now – the real start to the twenty-first century, where disruptive forces beyond our control have changed the landscape for good, and with technologies such as AI, blockchain, IoT and 5 G, ready to lead us onwards.

A tale of two planets – geographical and digital

The connectivity provided by the internet enabled the creation of a new type of citizen – the digital citizen. These digital citizens drifted together to form their own online tribes, forging connections with diverse groups of people who could be based anywhere around the world and enabling them to thrive in a way that they had never been able to in the real world.

Sometimes this was because they were viewed as outcasts in wider society, creating barriers in the real world to forming relationships. Other times it was because of their niche interests, where they just couldn't find people to engage with who were as passionate about them. Regardless of the underlying motivations, the online world changed the landscape and allowed people to have multiple identities – those in the real world and those in the virtual world.

As the technology has become more powerful these online worlds have become ever more impressive, evolving from bulletin boards, chatrooms and text-based games to immersive experiences based in virtual worlds like *World of Warcraft* and *Fortnite*, and high bandwidth video facilities available to many people via their smartphones.

Millions of people have also managed to make their living via their virtual existence on an ever-increasing number of platforms that allow people to magnify their voice or opinions, or find new ways to add value to commerce.

Regardless of where these virtual citizens live, they are all subject to the same real-world constraints – the geographical systems of currencies and laws in the physical world that underpin governments and society.

With the creation of monetary systems and services powered by decentralised technology, the opportunity to be a fully digital citizen emerges. One who can choose to embrace cryptocurrencies as their primary monetary system with its well-understood and transparent governance that is not subject to the whims of those with inflationary or deflationary powers at their disposal.

The ability to encode rules for digital citizens to abide by in smart contracts could ultimately provide law enforcement for the digital world too, supporting a fully digital existence. Naturally, the challenge of where someone can live in the real world that is fully supportive of such an existence remains to be seen; there will still need to be provisions for tax to ensure that revenues for government services can be collected. But it is likely we will see more libertarian individuals and, potentially, companies supportive of such a regime. In 2021, El Salvador was one such trailblazer, being the first country to adopt bitcoin as its legal tender.

When we might see such an autonomous future without human intervention remains a thought experiment, but it's fascinating to think about what could one day be possible with this new class of decentralised technologies emerging.

The emerging virtual state

Throughout the Covid-19 pandemic, one of the big beneficiaries has been cryptocurrency and blockchain technology. Huge amounts of funds have flowed into bitcoin, ether and other digital currencies from not just individuals but also large institutions. Companies such as MicroStrategy, Square and Tesla have taken significant positions in them, while other companies have been finding ways to cater for burgeoning demand from their customers.

Although much of the growth in digital assets is likely due to an ever-increasing number of speculators wanting to get exposure to the asset class, the majority of knowledge workers working from home during the pandemic have also been provided with the flexibility to scratch below the surface of crypto and blockchain. Another narrative could be emerging – that of the virtual state and citizens who become increasingly more convinced about the long-term viability of cryptocurrencies and blockchain technology to become a bedrock of their existence in society.

The earlier days of bitcoin and digital cash were very much driven as a libertarian movement, attracting individuals with an often more radical mindset – at one end the anti-state and government actor, and at the other the more moderate, focused on the right to privacy and control over how they conduct themselves online. The global financial crisis in 2008 triggered significant state-led bailouts by the Government, driving interest rates to record lows and fiscal stimulus in the form of quantitative easing. It was against this initial backdrop that bitcoin emerged in 2009. In addition to the above-mentioned attractions, digital libertarians were drawn to the notion of a decentralised currency – one that no government could exert control over and one that was immune to the whims of politicians and central bankers.

As hard as 2008 was on individuals, many western economies did manage to bounce back, albeit with growing budget deficits. As we headed into 2020, although there were murmurs of a virus that had emerged in China, things were generally rosy. In the first quarter of 2020, as the significance of Covid-19 started to hit and governments around the world taking various degrees of action, businesses started closing their doors and knowledge workers were sent home in droves.

Over the months that followed, individuals started adapting to life under lockdown and their individual circumstances varied greatly. Parents stuck at home found their already busy schedules becoming even busier, having to balance childcare, home learning and their jobs, while the young and those without additional caring responsibilities found themselves stuck at home with far more time on their hands then they were used to.

The combination of this additional free time and ability to work without someone looking over their shoulder has, for some, poured fuel onto a fire that was already burning brightly. Before the dotcom bubble burst in the early 2000s, a culture of day trading and speculating in stocks for a quick profit emerged among retail traders who had sophisticated trading tools they could use at home that historically had only been available to brokers. This created huge in-flows into equities, generating amazing returns for some and just as incredible losses for many others. We all know where we ended up then, but there were some key differences in that it affected mainly western economies.

China was yet to assert itself as the economic powerhouse it is now and Japan, previously one of the world's most admired economies, was still reeling from its lost decade of growth in the 1990s.

Now, over twenty years later, we find ourselves in a very different situation. Some of the hallmarks of the dotcom boom are present. A new class of retail speculators has emerged, but this time they have more time on their hands, more sophisticated tools and lower transaction costs with not just traditional equity markets, but also crypto. Many are saying that a huge bubble is emerging, but there's some interesting dynamics at play that I would argue mean this time it truly is different – some big changes are going to emerge (perhaps from the rubble following a collapse, but perhaps not).

Government deficits have ballooned to levels no one could have envisaged pre-Covid-19 and, unfortunately, we're not at the point yet where we know how the full implications of these emergency monetary policy measures are going to play out. What you can be sure of is that those fiat currencies that were used to fund government measures are not going to appreciate in value any time soon, which brings us onto the key discussion here – digital assets and the crypto state.

Covid-19 is the catalyst for change that has permanently shifted the opinion of many on cryptocurrency.

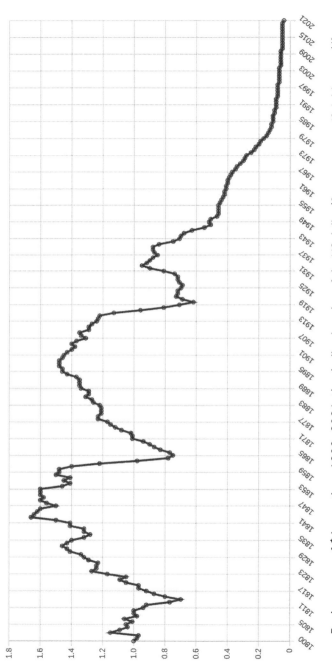

Buying power of $1 over time, 1800 – 2021: the decline in value of the US dollar (Source: www.officialdata.org)[42]

We'd seen previous cycles where there had been huge appreciation in the value of cryptocurrencies, followed by a crash in prices. Prior to late 2020, the last time we saw such enthusiasm was in 2017 when there was significant growth driven by ICO mania. Companies were being created backed by nothing more than a white paper outlining how they were going to disrupt an existing industry using decentralised technology, and people were piling into these ICOs with the promise of getting rich quickly with the surging demand for these projects. Much of this was driven by the digital tokenisation technology that came out of the Ethereum blockchain platform discussed in the previous chapter.

Anyone could, in effect, create their own tokens on the platform to represent fractional ownership of some good, be it another currency, loyalty points and, in the case of ICOs, utility tokens.

In 2017 this didn't end well. The price of bitcoin and ether (the cryptocurrency powering the Ethereum network which was supporting this ICO mania) appreciated significantly. There was huge growth of projects and companies launching ICOs, but many of them ended up being lemons as far as the investors in them were concerned. These projects' tokens ended up being worth far less than anticipated, or even worthless, while the projects themselves fell by the wayside due to bad luck or fraud, or remained stuck in obscurity with questionable technology to come out of them.

Back then, speculation in cryptocurrency and ICOs was the primary driver of the boom in cryptocurrency prices. This time around there is a degree of this, but the landscape has changed and expanded to be far broader than it ever was before.

First of all, the digital gold narrative has grown stronger for bitcoin, as adoption has grown due to its scarcity and limited supply. And, like gold, many see it as a hedge against inflation. As more people have started to appreciate the value of bitcoin and other digital assets, that has reinforced this view and there are increasingly more people subscribing to this narrative.

With Gen-Z[43] being mobile natives, the notion of a digital currency no doubt makes more sense to them than a physical yellow metal that has to be mined out of the ground, with its significant challenges with security, transportation and subdivision. Although bitcoin does suffer from some of these to a point, its digital nature certainly simplifies things.

The demand from the younger generation has seen many of the disruptive fintech businesses embracing digital currencies for their users, making it straightforward for them to gain exposure to this asset class in the same manner as they can with any traditional equity.

We've also seen money managers, the clients of wealth managers and customers of investment banks paying ever more attention to the returns being generated by this asset class and wanting to find ways to gain exposure. Thus large financial institutions have been scrambling to provide financial products, such as digital asset invest-ment trusts created by the likes of Greyscale, to cater for these snowballing demands, in turn creating more and more institutional interest.

Regulators around the world have been struggling to keep up with the innovations, and in some more extreme instances banning the holding of crypto assets, but in more moderate jurisdictions creating legislation to ensure that gains are treated like any other investable asset.

This insatiable demand, supported by more reliable and readily available on-ramps provided by crypto exchanges, coupled with generally widespread support from the legis-lature, has allowed the assets and the underlying technolo-gies to proliferate to a degree not seen previously.

As more and more people gain exposure to and start to understand these assets, they will also explore other ways they can use them. The innovations provided by DeFi to obtain new types of yield will draw more and more indi-viduals into them, incentivising exchanges to provide convenient bridges to these decentralised ecosystems and further reinforce the network effect associated with the blockchain networks where these innovations are being built.

But it's not just the crypto assets pulling people in. The creation of digital collectables and art via NFTs is casting the net of blockchain technology ever wider and inspiring the curious to find new ways in which to engage and add value through these ecosystems.

It doesn't stop there. As organisations invest in blockchain to help them streamline their supply chains, digitise their physical assets, reduce or even eliminate intermediaries from their value chains, the possibilities compound. Taking what started off as mainstream acceptance of cryptocurrencies and turning it into blockchain becoming a new foundational layer of the internet, brings us ever closer to truly decentralised virtual states.

Decentralised identity promises to address many of the problems sitting at the heart of the current generation of so-called free online platforms where the consumer is the product.

Why now is the right time

Perhaps some of what I've discussed here seems far-fetched, or you don't believe it could become a reality because of the control it would require those in power to relinquish. The point is not to convince you that there is one path to follow, but to make you aware of what's already happening with this technology so as to challenge your existing thinking of what's possible.

There are those who believe blockchain is a fringe technology, not ready for mainstream adoption. However, I doubt you are in that camp as you made it this far. You may, though, be unsure if now is the right time to scratch beneath the surface and see where it can take you. Fortunately, I will be providing you with everything you need to do to ensure that you can capitalise on this technology in a manner conducive to your business. We'll also discuss how you can convince your key stakeholders why now is the right time. Most importantly, the approach we present will not cause you to fall prey to the sunk-cost fallacy that has caused many a project to fail only once it has exhausted all available resources given to it.

Summary

One of the big beneficiaries of the Covid-19 global pandemic has been cryptocurrency and blockchain technology. Investments in and adoption of the technology have grown significantly.

We've seen huge growth in DeFi and NFTs during this period, helping to reinforce the network effect of blockchain.

In addition, innovations such as decentralised identity will help transition us away from Web 2.0 platforms where the user is the product.

PART TWO

THE JOURNEY

Undertaking any transformation requires you to embark on a journey, taking you to a new destination that opens doors to new opportunities.

The more disruptive the technology, the more interesting the journey is to get you to your destination.

In this part I'll be discussing the blockchain innovator's journey and the right path to follow to ensure you reach your desired destination.

6

The Blockchain Innovator's Journey

Now we've covered a number of the fundamentals and provided wider perspective on blockchain and DLT technology, you're probably thinking, 'This is great, but how does it apply to my business? We can't afford to launch decentralised applications that use decentralised governance structures, or start using cryptocurrencies to fund new projects. We have a reputation to uphold, existing customers to service and quarterly targets to hit to keep our shareholders happy.'

And you'd be absolutely right. These are some of the fundamentals that drive your business – you can't suddenly drop everything, roll the dice and immerse yourself 100% in blockchain.

But what you should be doing at the very least is exploring what your competitors are doing, what's possible for your business and how it can help you challenge the status quo. We'll go into detail on how you can do exactly that, but first it's important to discuss the broader framework you can use to approach this technology.

Given their disruptive nature, blockchain and decentralised technologies require a somewhat different approach up front in assessing the ways in which they can impact your business, both from a threats and opportunity perspective, and in how to apply them to your organisation. But once you have found the appropriate destination, the path to take you there is less radical.

The blockchain innovator's journey is split into three distinct phases, supporting you from ideation all the way through to a live platform supporting your customers at scale. These phases are outlined below.

The three phases

Discovery   Design   Deploy

Phase 1: Discovery

The discovery phase is made up of two steps. It starts by identifying where this technology can bring the most value to your business. Once potential targets are identified, you may subsequently undertake a proof of concept, or proto-typing exercise. This provides an opportunity to under-stand and validate what's possible within the context of your organisation and the benefits it can bring.

The key outcome of this phase are learnings that you can bring with you into the next phase.

Phase 2: Design

Having identified and validated a potential opportunity, the second phase is where you explore in detail how you can take what you learned in the first phase and build out a minimum viable product to support your business objectives.

During this phase you will need not only to focus on the product requirements, but also on obtaining stakeholder support and engaging with potential customers to bring them on board as early as possible. You'll also need to consider governance and other items, as blockchain appli-cations have their own unique nuances and challenges.

This will be supported by a sound go-to-market strategy to support the launch of this offer.

Phase 3: Deploy

The final phase is where all of the planning and execu-tion comes together, resulting in your bringing your new offer to market. The way in which you do this will vary from organisation to organisation, but this is the phase where your product gets launched and is used by real customers.

The product will evolve and continue to be refined over time, but at this stage you should treat it in a similar manner to your other business applications, with it addressing the problem that you set out to solve when you first embarked on this journey.

What if my destination changes?

This approach allows you to sharpen your focus as you progress. You start off with a macro perspective of your business. From here you establish where the most potentially rewarding areas to focus on are. You then identify a single, smaller opportunity to validate facts and your thinking (discovery) and, if this is successful, you start to elaborate on what you've already done, investing more resources in it incrementally as you build confidence that you're on the right track (design). Then, as the stars align and you start to demonstrate tangible value, you'll start finding more advocates and fewer naysayers.

You're not going all in from the start; you want to build momentum gradually, only taking the opportunity to market once you have validation from real customers (deploy).

Think about when you're planning a trip. You start by establishing the goal of the trip (the problem or an opportunity). Are you planning to undertake a specific activity such as skiing or snowboarding, or perhaps just some winter sun? As you research the different options you start to identify a country or region that works for you, refining the scope in the process.

Next you start researching the towns or resorts you'd like to stay in, and the methods by which you can travel there, designing the specific details of your holiday. However, you are not committed to this holiday yet; you can still tweak all the details, until you're ready to pay your deposits for your flights, accommodation and activities.

Finally, with everything locked in, you just count down to your trip. You've done a lot of research and planning to get here, perhaps done some training to get you in shape for some of the activities you'll be undertaking. You're putting yourself out there, in unfamiliar territory, but feel ready to embrace the change as you've had plenty of time to plan and prepare for this adventure.

Over the coming chapters we'll be unpacking each of these phases in detail and providing you with many of the resources you need to maximise your chance of success by embracing this technology.

If you're already well versed in technical project delivery, especially with emergent technologies, you may want to skip through certain sections of the next four chapters of the book, as some of what I cover will likely be familiar ground to you. I encourage you, however, not to skip over any of the blockchain-specific considerations that I outline.

Summary

The blockchain innovator's journey is divided into three phases:

- It starts with the discovery phase where you identify a suitable opportunity and undertake a proof of concept (PoC) or prototyping exercise.

- This leads into the design phase, where you build on what you learned in the first phase and create a minimum viable product to support your business objectives.

- Finally, during the deploy phase you bring your new offer to market and have it used by real customers.

7

Discovery Part One

As you begin the first phase of your journey, discovery, it's important to carve out space from your schedule to start immersing yourself more in the world of blockchain and DLT so you can appreciate how quickly the landscape is evolving.

In this chapter I will be providing ways in which you can approach this to ensure that you are well placed and have the right mindset to identify the right opportunities for your organisation.

This work will provide the foundations upon which you start your exploration.

Disruptive forces

To create something disruptive, you need to free your mind from the everyday noise and distractions around you. Innovation comes from creativity; if you can't engage with your creative brain you're going to struggle to figure out how blockchain can benefit your organisation.

If you want to find new opportunities for your business, outdo your competitors, or solve some of the internal technology problems that are the bane of your life, you've got to get out of your comfort zone to find inspiration. You need to be brave enough to be creative.

Of course you've got a hundred and one different things on your mind at any one time, and you can't just drop everything to start being more creative, but there are things you can do that will get you there.

Think about some of the biggest breakthroughs that have happened in the last twenty years. Spotify and Netflix turned the consumption of music and television on its head. Imagine telling someone in the 1990s that in the 2020s people would have a back catalogue of most of the world's music, or an endless library of TV shows and films at their disposal for $10 per month. No one would believe you. Businesses like Spotify and Netflix didn't just innovate, they changed the parameters of the game. And that is exactly what blockchain is doing.

Hence you need to shift your mind into a parallel universe to start thinking about what's possible. Fortunately, in the world we live in today, you can find inspiration in more places than ever before; you just need to be disciplined enough to carve out time to engage with them.

Get inspired

Inspiration is the cricket ball that hits you outside of your peripheral vision. Once you see the ball, you know people are playing cricket, but you didn't see it coming.

Let's go back to the 1990s again and ask people how music or television could improve as a medium – most people would have requested more diverse content and more channels. The idea of making all content available instantly would have required too great a conceptual leap to even cross their mind, but in hindsight it seems obvious. This is what's so powerful about the most ground-breaking ideas and innovations – they seem obvious once you're aware of them.

So, what are some of the best ways to get inspired? Start by carving out some time to take your mind off your day-to-day work. Everyone has their own ways of doing this, but one of the most reliable ways is to get out of the house or office for a walk. Often I'll listen to a podcast – for some ideas check out the resources at the end of the book. Other times I want my mind to be free to wander, or perhaps I meditate. Make sure you're not getting distracted by your phone or notifications during this time.

Also, don't fall into the trap of consuming only content that is relevant to your own industry, or just focusing on blockchain. Getting ideas from subjects outside your core expertise can be very powerful in seeing new opportunities. It's this crossover where some fantastic disruption happens. In his 2005 Stanford commencement speech, Steve Jobs discussed how attending calligraphy classes in college led him to learn about typefaces, which led him to design 'beautiful typography' for the Mac.[44]

Try, too, to ensure you're getting the sleep you need. Sleep deprivation drastically reduces your brain's executive function, which is responsible for tasks such as focus, self-control and creativity. If you need convincing of the importance of this, I implore you to read Matthew Walker's excellent book on the subject.[45]

What about those pressing issues on your mind that you really can't shake off? Sometime you just need to clear your head, which is where some more intensive exercise helps. Personally, I enjoying practising Brazilian jiu-jitsu – there is no better way of being present than fighting for your life in a safe environment.

The restrictions that the Covid-19 pandemic has placed on everyday life mean that you don't always have the option of meeting people, but if you can immerse yourself among a different group of peers, or attend events such as meet-ups or conferences that enable you to see what other people and organisations are doing with blockchain, this can be another great source of inspiration.

CASE STUDY: BLOCKCHAIN EVENTS

Web3 Labs has been running a monthly blockchain event since July 2017. The Enterprise Ethereum Alliance Virtual Meetup brings together leading blockchain technologists and business people to listen to engaging talks and network with like-minded peers from companies including Microsoft, Santander and ING. Originally a face-to-face event in London, the switch to remote working caused by Covid-19 transitioned it to a virtual event.

To ensure that people still have networking opportunities, small virtual rooms between talks give attendees a chance to meet someone new, extending their network.

You can join the group at meetup.com/eea-london. Talks from previous events are available on the Web3 Labs YouTube channel at www.youtube.com/c/web3labs.

By getting into the habit of making time to find inspiration in your everyday life, you will open your mind up to a new world of possibility. Your brain will not only reward you with endorphins as new connections are made between synapses, but you'll also start appreciating just how much progress has been made in the past decade alone with decentralised technology, and why the buzz around it is justified.

I provide a number of free podcast and video recommendations in the resources at the end of this book which I encourage you listen to or watch. They'll help broaden your perspectives on everything that is happening in the space. You may find yourself sucked down the rabbit hole, but trust me, it's a lot of fun, with some incredible and very smart people working on some big problems.

As you embark on your journey you no doubt will encounter critics, but remember the words of Dita von Teese: 'You can be the most delicious peach in the world, but some people just don't like peaches.'

A solution looking for a problem

Perhaps you've heard of people refer to blockchain as a solution looking for a problem, or the drill in Theodore Levitt's famous quote, 'People don't want quarter-inch drill bits. They want quarter-inch holes.'

Not everyone knows what they want to do with their drill, but people are also subject to a whole number of different mental biases that prevent them from seeing what's possible. If finding new ways to solve existing problems wasn't important, or improving the tools that we already have wasn't necessary, as a society we would still be stuck somewhere in the Neolithic age.[46]

As you start to understand what's possible and appreciate what's happening on the cutting edge in areas such as DeFi and NFTs, you need to find a way to make this relevant to your business in an impactful way. Your view from 10,000 feet may feel like a long way from the ground and you're struggling to see where you'll land, so start thinking about the threats and opportunities that face your organisation, and how you might respond to or capture them.

Ensure you find people to collaborate with on this. I'm always amazed by the difference it makes when I externalise ideas for feedback from someone else. Don't make the mistake of keeping things to yourself, find people you can bounce ideas off. The sooner the better, so you don't go off on a tangent that misses the mark.

If you are not yourself working within the innovation function of your organisation, find people that are. Blockchain and decentralised technologies are likely to have come up on their radar and there are bound to be many willing collaborators. These groups will probably already have defined an innovation process for your business, along with checkpoints and committees that will make the whole process of how to approach a new initiative significantly simpler than trying to create one yourself. Alternatively, ask any of the teams or individuals reporting to you. If you feel stuck finding collaborators, try creating a blockchain special interest group that meets up once a month for an hour to discuss the opportunities and latest developments. People with aligned interests will quickly emerge from the woodwork.

Once you have some collaborators, you can start to identify the potential problems and opportunities that are relevant to your organisation. These typically fall into two categories: the obvious problems and the not so obvious ones.

The obvious problems

These are the significant problems that probably impact your business time and time again, with no end in sight. They include items such as the following.

- Service availability
  - Single points of failure in centralised systems such as identity management and access control impacting key services

- Data quality and provenance
  - Data being duplicated time and again across different silos; questionable accuracy of data feeding from systems of record
  - Lack of trust in the data being presented or reported across business units or externally
  - Brittle reconciliation processes throughout the organisation between business units

- Intermediaries
  - Reliance on a high number of intermediaries for core services
  - Complex, transactional business processes that span multiple entities, both internal and external

- Competitor pressures
  - Competitors and rivals marching ahead with innovations you don't have time to think about or cannot keep up with

- Regulatory pressures
  - An ever-increasing burden of new legislation that you need to comply with

The less obvious problems or opportunities

However, issues or potential opportunities are also happening under the radar that you may not even have the time to think about currently, including:

- The potential for decentralisation to displace intermediaries you rely on currently

- Digitisation of existing physical or digital assets

- Emerging consumer demand for cryptocurrencies

- Opportunities to release exclusive or promotional NFTs

- Innovations in decentralised identity that remove the need for centralised identity management solutions

- Innovations in decentralised finance, such as the trading of assets, insurance and lending

I encourage you to capture as many of them as possible. Try to prioritise them to find the emerging common themes or issues.

Identifying and finding these different categories can also be complemented by other approaches you can try, including:

- Ideation or discovery sessions

- Internal competitions or even hackathons with prizes for the best ideas

- Interviewing customers about their significant pain points and challenges

You want to create a machine to generate ideas, rather than being an individual creating them in isolation.

Turning inside out

Although easy to frame as threats, many of these also present great opportunities that can open up entirely new business opportunities, because decentralisation turns businesses inside out, with blockchain providing the layer of trust between participants. It is incredibly powerful.

For example, you have a complex supply chain that entails multiple organisations transporting some goods from A to B. If the key event records of that supply chain live on a blockchain instead of as a brittle daisy chain of connections spanning multiple organisations' systems of record, as is typically the case, everyone has access to the same world view. Straightaway you can see how this drastically reduces the amount of communication that needs to take place between parties and eliminates a lot of the friction that exists between participants.

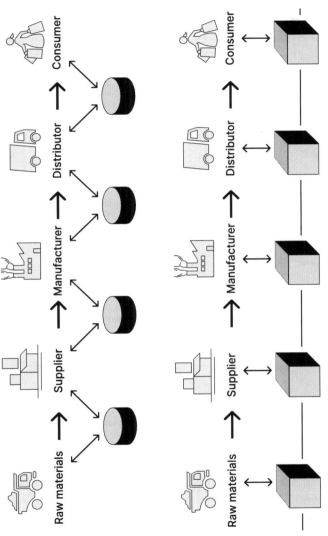

Raw materials → Supplier → Manufacturer → Distributor → Consumer

A traditional supply chain versus one underpinned by a blockchain

CASE STUDY: AWARD-WINNING SUPPLY CHAIN INNOVATION

Microsoft has used decentralised technology to great effect with its cloud supply chain blockchain initiative, which was awarded the prestigious 'Supply Chain Breakthrough of the Year' and 'Process or Technology Innovation of the Year' by Gartner.[47]

This platform provides mine-to-data centre traceability for parts of its commodities value chain, starting with solid-state drives (SSD) and dynamic random access memory (DRAM) components.

The savings realised through the platform are estimated at $50 million per year, due to the integrity of transactions and reduced pricing errors.

I encourage you to contemplate the viewpoint that opposes how you think about parts of your organisation currently. 'What if everything we do internally as a business was available externally?' This may be a more extreme way to think about your organisation, but I guarantee it will help you to see the new efficiencies it can bring and opportunities it can provide.

I'm not saying you have to do this to embrace blockchain properly, but this sort of inside-out thinking, coupled with how you could tie it up with well-established blockchain innovations such as cryptocurrencies and tokens, NFTs and DeFi, is an incredibly powerful toolkit.

Naturally, your organisation contains a lot of sensitive information that you have a duty to protect, be this customer data, intellectual property or that related to your fiduciary duties. It would be foolish of me to suggest anything that could put this in jeopardy. But these are merely thought experiments to open your eyes to what's possible, and when it comes to building a real application using this technology, we will ensure the relevant precautions and security measures are in place to fully protect any sensitive data you may have.

Further inspiration

Regardless of your industry, you can find an abundance of information on how companies are adopting the technology and the various use cases they are focusing on. You will also start to appreciate the parallel ecosystems that are spinning up in the decentralised space; depending on your industry these may be relevant for you.

Armed with this information you can start to make the connections that exist between the threats and opportunities that you have gathered, and start identifying ways in which blockchain and DLT could benefit areas of your organisation. Then you can start formulating a concrete plan on how best to exploit this technology.

The key thing is that you've found what you believe to be a valid opportunity to explore further.

CASE STUDY: EXECUTIVE WORKSHOPS

Some organisations we work with at Web3 Labs are clear on what they want to achieve with blockchain when they first approach us. Others need help to understand the landscape and identify the opportunities best suited to their organisation.

For those organisations that need guidance, we provide executive workshops that help identify the right blockchain opportunities to support digital transformation initiatives.

During these workshops we help leadership teams and executives:

- Understand the blockchain and DLT landscape
- Identify business threats and opportunities
- Align with the right business opportunity, highlighting key projects and innovations
- Define goals, objectives and next steps

The end result being that they are clear on how best their organisation can exploit opportunities with blockchain.

Summary

The first part of the discovery process entails finding the right business opportunity to target. Try to adopt a more creative mindset and find people to work with.

Useful sources of inspiration include:

- Walking and listening to podcasts

- Attending industry events or meet-ups

- Getting enough sleep, meditation and exercise

- Learning about subjects outside your core area of expertise

There are a number of places you can find potential collaborators:

- In the teams or individuals reporting to you

- In your innovation department

- By joining or establishing blockchain special interest groups

To identify suitable opportunities, try applying inside-out thinking to see how parts of your business could work differently. Other approaches to try include:

- Ideation or discovery sessions

- Internal competitions or even hackathons with prizes for the best ideas

- Interviewing customers about their significant pain points and challenges

8
Discovery Part Two

As you become more familiar with the world of blockchain and decentralised technology, you will appreciate the great number of potential opportunities it can provide.

The first part of the discovery process entails finding the right sources of inspiration and identifying business problems or opportunities to exploit. The second stage is validating these findings and formulating a plan for some initial work with this technology. In this chapter I will expand on how you can approach this.

An evidence-based approach

To decide how best to proceed with the discovery phase of a process, it is important to embrace an evidence-based approach in defining the goal or hypothesis that we wish to achieve. The concept of evidence-based decision-making came from the medical profession in the 1980s, where the idea of using the best currently available evidence should be adopted in making decisions that affect the care of individual patients, as opposed to just blindly following the opinions of experts. The effectiveness of evidence-based approaches has gained significant traction in recent years outside of the medical profession, with governments, businesses and policymakers all looking to find ways to utilise evidence-based approaches in their deployment of resources.

For instance, in 2018 the US Government passed a new law in the form of its Foundations for Evidence-Based Policymaking Act to require the federal government to modernise its data management practices – testament to its influence in supporting wide-reaching decisions and policy making.[48]

From a practical perspective what this means is that in order to follow an evidence-based approach, you should consider carefully the different sources of information you use to inform your thinking, and formulate a clear question or hypothesis that frames the problem you are trying to solve at the outset. Armed with this information, you ensure you use the right sources of data to support your initial line of questioning.

It is upon this foundation that we want to proceed within the discovery phase of the project, so that not only do we create a goal or hypothesis that we wish to achieve, but also that we can test it and apply a degree of scepticism to the result. This ensures that when we review what we have achieved we can be pragmatic about the best next steps to take (if any).

This work can be split into four phases:

- Align
- Assess
- Review
- Next steps

Align

Start by bringing together all of your learnings so far about blockchain and the key threats and opportunities facing your organisation. You want to identify and frame what the core problem or opportunity is that you want to focus on first.

In addition to speaking to relevant business stakeholders, this should be underpinned by appropriate research from quality sources that provide information that is relevant to your business or your goals.

Research can be split into two types of evidence: filtered and unfiltered. The robustness of these different sources of evidence is captured in the following image.

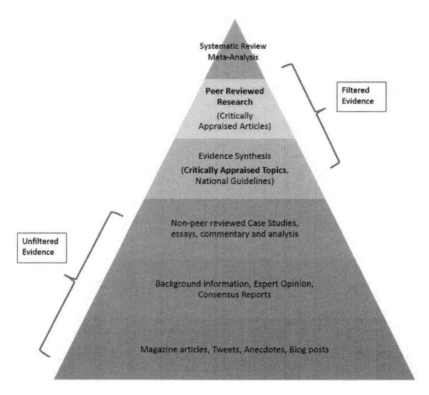

Filtered vs unfiltered evidence (Source: Naseem Naqvi and Mureed Hussain, 'Evidence- Based Blockchain: Findings from a Global Study of Blockchain Projects and Start-up Companies')[49]

1. Filtered evidence comes from trusted academic sources, such as peer reviewed journals or conferences. Examples include The Directory of Open Access Journals,[50] Google Scholar and SSRN.[51]

2. Unfiltered evidence comes from non-peer reviewed sources such as blog articles, social media and news sites. Hence you need to prioritise filtered research if you wish to use an evidence-based approach.

Next you need to figure out what goals and objectives you'd most like to achieve with this initial piece of work and what are your success criteria. This is so that your team can be clear on what a successful outcome looks like, to decide if the work warrants further exploration beyond this phase. Therefore, you want to try to find evidence from filtered or peer reviewed sources here, to ensure you have more quality sources to support your goals.

You want to focus on goals and objectives that are unlikely to require support from additional stakeholders or teams to demonstrate. Aim to ring-fence this work, so that you can rapidly produce a tangible result, typically in a six to twelve-week time horizon.

The types of goals at this phase could include:

- Comparing our existing data storage infrastructure to understand if using a blockchain or DLT platform would provide improved data integrity and availability guarantees for our customers and reduce the data reconciliation burden in our organisation

- Trialling if using a smart contract platform will provide improved trust and transparency of the settlement lifecycle, whilst also reducing operating costs we bear in using them (instead of relying on an intermediary for our asset settlement activities)

- Testing if, compared with our existing paper-based supply chain, a blockchain or DLT platform will reduce costs, save time and increase customer satisfaction with our products

- Considering if the tokenisation of some business assets using smart contracts provides us with a mechanism to fractionalise ownership of them and enable us to provide greater liquidity of our balance sheet, reducing the time and costs associated with holding these assets

- Comparing if a blockchain can protect us against data falsification and provide these reports in a near real-time manner against our existing manually generated, monthly P&L reports from our subsidiaries.

The PCIO framework (Problem – Comparison – Intervention – Outcomes) from the *Journal of the British Blockchain Association* provides an approach that can help to inform this more precise line of questioning. It is summarised below.

WHAT IS THE PROBLEM?

Q1: Is there a clearly defined problem to be solved?

Q2: What is the evidence that the problem exists?
(Who is affected? Who is talking about it?)

Q3: How significant is the problem? (Extent and magnitude)

WHAT ARE THE EXISTING SOLUTIONS?
(COMPARISON/CONTROL)

Q4: What are the existing solutions available
to address the problem?

Q5: What are the results/outcomes
of the existing solutions/systems?

Q6: Are these critically evaluated? Are the results published?

WHAT IS THE NEW INTERVENTION?

Q7: What is the intervention? Why and how is it different
from other solutions?

Q8: Is there scientific evidence to back up the intervention?

Q9: Intervention critically evaluated?
If so, by whom and what are the outcomes?

WHAT ARE THE OUTCOMES?

Q10: What are the key outcomes of interest?

Q11: Have the results shown an objective improvement
in outcomes?

Q12: Outcomes independently evaluated or
critically appraised (peer reviewed)?

Evidence assessment framework for blockchain applications
(Source: Naseem Naqvi and Mureed Hussain, 'Evidence- Based
Blockchain: Findings from a Global Study of Blockchain Projects and
Start-up Companies')[52]

You should capture your goals or problem statement somewhere before undertaking the project, and define and capture process flows using sequence diagrams or similar, to clarify the different actors that you wish to represent and the manner in which they engage with each other and the platform.

This should not be a lengthy document, just one that captures the essence of what you're trying to achieve with the key details provided in a clear and simple format.

It should also be shared with relevant stakeholders so they have a clear understanding of the work that is being performed and its criteria for success.

Assess

This phase is about understanding the feasibility of what you are trying to achieve. You can take various approaches, typically a feasibility study or the building of a prototype or proof of concept (PoC) that can be used to validate the goals and objectives that you set out to proceed.

For example, if you are evaluating different blockchain platforms, you might run a series of tests against some criteria you've defined, such as how one deploys a decentralised application on the platform and how it can be subsequently managed. Or perhaps you want to create a decentralised application that demonstrates a subset of the features you'd like to explore in a controlled environment. It is open-ended at this stage.

Six weeks is the ideal duration for this initial piece of work, but it may make sense to extend this up to twelve depending on the complexity of what you're trying to achieve. Any longer and it starts to look less like an exploratory activity and more like building out a real product.

You also want a single team of between two and five people working on this initiative. Weekly review meetings are essential to keep various stakeholders and sponsors up to date with progress.

Regardless of exactly how you go about assessing the feasibility of what you're trying to achieve, it's important to appease your inner scientist and ensure that the team keep the original problem statement front of mind, which was outlined via the goals and objectives of this project.

CASE STUDY: PROOF OF CONCEPTS

At Web3 Labs we regularly discuss different approaches to proof of concept exercises with our prospective clients. The needs of one organisation vary significantly from another's, which is reflected in the different types of engagement we are brought in to undertake.

Recent examples of proof of concepts we've proposed include:

- Simulating existing types of financial debt asset using a DeFi protocol
- Creation of a decentralised solution marketplace

- Demonstrating smart contract interoperability approaches between different blockchain technologies

Although the goals of these projects differ, they all provide good opportunities to demonstrate the viability of a concept, building on top of blockchain platforms before potentially undertaking a more significant build-out. This ensures we are establishing the feasibility of the project as early as possible.

Evaluating blockchain projects and technologies

You can take a number of due diligence steps to evaluate blockchain platforms or technologies before you undertake any serious assessment of them, especially if you are considering a more cutting-edge solution. Unlike the naive ICO investors of the past, this will help ensure that you don't end up holding a lemon:

- Does the project have a white paper? If so, does it read well and make sense?

- Do the key staff of the company have LinkedIn and Twitter profiles? Are they publishing genuinely helpful content, or just promoting a token or cryptocurrency?

- Is their experience on LinkedIn indicative of having the credentials to perform this role?

- Is the documentation portal of the project accurate and up to date?

- Are the GitHub repositories associated with the organisation at github.com being updated regularly by the people associated with the project? Is a community engaging with them, and are they responding in a timely manner?

- Is there a public chatroom such as a Discord or Telegram group? Are people discussing meaningful topics there, or just token prices?

- Are there filtered sources of research that reference this project?

If reading technical documentation or looking at GitHub repositories is out of your reach, most competent technologists in your organisation should have the ability to substantiate these for you.

Public or private?

A consideration that's likely to come up at this point is the type of blockchain network you want to work with. In Chapter 2 we looked at the different public and private blockchain networks.

If you do want to work with a public blockchain network, you should always start with a test blockchain network, or testnet. Although thus far we have spoken about public blockchain networks in a singular capacity, in reality they all have at least one, often many versions of them are available for testing. These testnets provide freely available test versions of their cryptocurrencies for users to work with them in a safe environment for experimentation.

The main network that does require cryptocurrency to transact with them is referred to as the mainnet.

Because private blockchain networks offer greater flexibility and control, and don't require real cryptocurrency to transact with them, many organisations start with them to run their initial PoCs – it is far easier to transition from a private network to a public network than vice versa.

That said, it is important to consider what the right longer-term place for your application will be. In private consortia, remaining on a private blockchain may make sense. This will require additional overhead from a governance perspective, which we discuss in the next chapter. However, much as technologies like virtual private networks (VPNs) allow companies to run infrastructure that resides on top of the internet, privacy techniques are evolving that allow organisations to plug their applications into public blockchain networks. One such example is the Baseline Protocol, which provides a common frame of reference for systems of record.[53]

The open and transparent nature of public blockchain networks often does not meet the requirements that larger organisations have concerning privacy, permissioning and identity. Businesses want to know who they are serving with their products and services, but don't necessarily want their competitors to know, and the pseudoanony-mous nature of participants on public networks may not be appropriate, especially if they need to adhere to consid-erations such as KYC. As the technology matures this is becoming less of an issue, and although readily available access to public blockchain networks via the internet is very attractive, many organisations are not yet willing to embrace the degree of data transparency required with many public blockchain applications.

It's important that you retain an open mindset about using public blockchain infrastructure. You may feel that the public networks do not meet your needs yet, or that they're too open. However, this space is evolving rapidly so you should not discount the potential they can offer. Remember – you need to think about which processes within your organisation you can turn inside out.

Review

Once you've completed what you set out to assess, you're now ready to wrap up the discovery phase by reviewing what you have achieved. Hopefully plenty of learnings have come out of this work, and you're clear on potential next steps.

Applying some common project success criteria supported by your evidence-based approach can provide a useful framework for capturing these learnings:

- Did you capture quality results?

- Was the scope adequate and did you achieve what you set out to?

- Was it achieved on schedule?

- Was the budget adhered to?

- Was the customer or client satisfied with the result?

- Is the team that performed the work satisfied with the result?

- Has the quality of the result met stakeholder expectations?

- How do your results stack up against your original problem statement or goal?

Questioning why you achieved the result you did for each of these criteria will help you unearth the specific details underpinning your learnings. In addition, the gaps in your solution that were identified as a result of this work can be taken on board should a subsequent iteration take place.

These learnings should be both quantitative and qualitative in nature as they provide strong data points that can be presented as facts to stakeholders in a presentation or report. This ensures the outcome of the work is well understood and it's clear what has and hasn't worked.

Depending on the goals of this phase, it may also make sense to prepare some external communications to share with a wider audience of what you achieved (presuming you're happy with the result). This is often in the form of a press release or blog post and can help ensure the information being presented is factual in nature. The gold standard here would be to get the results published in a peer reviewed journal or at a conference to support subsequent evidence-based research. However, there may be challenges depending on commercial sensitivities and the willingness of stakeholders to support this.

Next steps

In an ideal world your next steps would build upon what you've created thus far and justify moving into the next phase But it's important to be realistic about what you've achieved, so they may not. Typically, you will face one of the following options:

1. Move forward into the next phase – design

2. Repeat the discovery process, realigning with new goals and objectives

3. Realise that blockchain isn't right and won't benefit your organisation

Regardless of what your exercise achieved, by applying the methods here you will have approached the discovery phase in a manner that is most conducive to providing learnings for your organisation.

CASE STUDY: EQUIPMENT FINANCING POC

Equipment Connect is a marketplace for business equipment and associated services, allowing small businesses to source, finance and manage equipment digitally on one (web) app.[54]

The market for financing business equipment is often paper-based, inefficient and opaque, so approving and processing transactions can be slow with much intermediation. Although the industry is worth €300 billion in Europe, many funders rely on legacy tech that generally isn't well integrated with vendors selling the equipment and data providers. As a result, many traditional funders carry the burden of excessive back office, trustee and reconciliation costs and are exposed to fraud because of the fragmented nature of the record keeping.

Equipment Connect are the first fintech platform to fully digitise the equipment finance user flow, integrating small equipment suppliers and their customers into a multi-funder leasing marketplace.

On the back of an Innovate UK award to increase data integrity and reduce risk of fraud, Web3 Labs partnered with Equipment Connect to create a solution that would store digital fingerprints of financing agreements on a blockchain. This work was performed as a proof of concept, and proved successful in demonstrating how the technology could be used to streamline and mitigate against fraudulent activities through the equipment financing process.

It enabled Equipment Connect to learn first-hand how its platform could embrace the many benefits of blockchain in its digital marketplace, not only to increase trust between different funders but also to ensure greater confidence and fluidity in the title transfer process.

Blockchain principles for success

You may feel like you still have gaps in your knowledge or within your organisation of exactly how to go about approaching blockchain projects.

With this in mind, we created a number of guiding principles for successful blockchain deployments. These principles can be useful when undertaking a proof of concept exercise (and more in-depth blockchain projects) to give you the best chance of success.

The principles will help you to select the right:

- Target use case

- Team

- Technology

If you'd like to learn more about these considerations, I encourage you to attend one of our webinars on the principles of successful blockchain deployments. You can sign up at web3labs.com/principles-webinar.

You can also download our free e-book, *Principles of Successful Blockchain Deployments*, at web3labs.com/ resources, which includes a number of case studies that may provide further inspiration.

Summary

The second part of the discovery phase entails:

- Aligning the goals and objectives for a project
- Assessment via a feasibility study or building a PoC or prototype
- Reviewing what you've learned based on your original success criteria
- Identifying next steps

You should try to adopt an evidence-based approach to researching and framing your problem statement or goals. This will help you to follow a more precise line of questioning during this phase.

For a proof of concept exercise:

- Aim for six, but up to twelve weeks in duration.
- Put in place a team of two to five staff.
- Hold weekly review meetings to keep various stakeholders and sponsors up to date with progress.

- You will need to decide whether to use a public or private blockchain and you may want to undertake a brief due diligence of the chosen platform if it's one of the less established offerings.

When reviewing your project, you should ask the following questions:

- Did you capture quality results?

- Was the scope adequate and did you achieve what you set out to?

- Was it achieved on schedule?

- Was the budget adhered to?

- Was the customer or client satisfied with the result?

- Is the team that performed the work satisfied with the result?

- Has the quality of the result met stakeholder expectations?

- Were there any gaps in the final report or solution?

- How do you results stack up against your original problem statement or goal?

9
Design

When we enter the design phase, we are creating the foundations upon which we build out our solution. We develop upon what we learned in our discovery phase and start designing the full platform solution. In this phase we also build the initial version of our application, engage key stakeholders and plan our go-to-market strategy to support our deployment.

This preparation will help to minimise issues when it comes to the application deployment phase, which comes next.

The goal is to have something tangible that you can start putting in front of real customers, internal and/or external, by the end of this phase.

Incorporate learnings

The discovery phase enabled you to validate your initial goals and objectives for what could be achieved using blockchain technology, to address an existing problem or a new opportunity for your organisation. Now you're ready to sharpen your focus and start building out a platform or application to drive change.

At this point you should establish a clearer vision of what it is you're trying to achieve. It should be underpinned by clear success criteria that support the goals and objectives of the business problem or opportunity you are addressing, and you will no doubt need to adhere to internal processes.

The items that we discuss here are broad themes and principles you'll need to consider as you progress further through this phase.

Stakeholder and customer engagement

To expand the scope of what you wish to achieve, you will inevitably need to bring key business stakeholders on board. Having strategic support, ideally at the executive level, will help ensure that you're not facing an uphill battle as you move through this phase.

You don't want to be wasting time here – the right level of support is especially important because the true potential of disruptive technologies often isn't fully understood and can be too easily dismissed as inferior compared with the status quo. We discuss exactly how you can pitch block-chain to get this support later in this book.

You also need to think about your customers, who may be within another business unit or part of your organisation, or external. The key is to find a few customers (ideally three to keep it manageable) that you can work with early on, who can validate your assumptions and provide feedback on an ongoing basis.

This engagement should happen regularly, ideally weekly. It should include the sharing of information such as learnings so far. You should also share prototypes as they are created, and demos as soon as they are possible. Ensure you take on board and address any concerns or questions they raise.

Having this support will ensure you're building for the right audience and not making assumptions about your customers' wants and needs.

Architecture

Start creating alignment by sharing the vision of the platform with the technical teams, which should help provide clarity on what the business wishes to achieve with the implementation and provide a roadmap for the delivery.

The type of considerations the technology teams will want to address include:

- Blockchain network configuration and deployment
- Smart contract design and responsibilities
- Front-end design and user experience (UX)
- Blockchain integration services
- Data caching and reporting services
- Third-party or other application integrations
- Functional versus non-functional requirements
- Identity and access control

These can be captured in a variety of formats such as:

- User stories
- Sequence diagrams
- Architecture diagrams
- User interface mock-ups

Try to engage with end-customers when creating some of these assets, because the user experience will directly affect them. It's better to get their input before any code starts being written.

Try and keep these reference documents as simple as possible and in a place they can be readily accessed, such as a knowledge-sharing and collaboration tool. You should avoid having a lengthy architecture document that goes out of date as the system quickly evolves, which it will.

White papers and token sales

Many projects and protocols targeting public blockchains commence life as a white paper, where it is presented in a similar manner to a scientific paper, but without the formal peer review process behind it.

This approach was used by both the Bitcoin and Ethereum networks, and a multitude of projects since. It's usually used to generate interest in the protocol or application being delivered prior to fundraising via a token sale, as we discussed in Chapter 4. The reason why white papers are so popular in the space is that they allow project teams to go into greater levels of depth about how they plan to achieve their goals, which enables more scrutiny by readers. More traditional assets such as investor decks typically are more high level and, given that these teams are trying to drum up public interest in their proposal, a white paper's specificity helps legitimise what the project team is trying to achieve.

Unless your organisation has ambitions to raise investor funds via a token sale and launch a public-facing block-chain protocol, a white paper is less likely to be an appropriate route, as your organisation probably already has documentation standards by which to abide.

Additionally, if your company is public and wishes to launch a public-facing blockchain project that is underpinned by a utility token, there are considerations for how the distribution of such assets could impact existing shareholders, which is likely to be a non-trivial consideration. Plus, there are a number of regulatory and jurisdiction considerations with respect to how you approach token sales that require good legal representation. Such legal representation is absolutely critical if you wish to move forward with a token sale in the current regulatory environment.

Trust the machine

One of the mistakes we see again and again in a blockchain application is that the blockchain or distributed ledger component is treated as nothing more than a database technology for data storage and retrieval. If you find yourself going down this path, you are probably missing the point.

We discussed previously the idea of how decentralisation enables you to turn your business inside out – think about the possibilities that open up to your customers if they are presented with the same interface to your platform as would be available internally. It is this common interface that can be provided by the blockchain.

You need to consider what business logic you want to encapsulate in a smart contract. This requires you to trust the blockchain, which is likely to require a conceptual leap in your thinking.

In a traditional, centralised system, you are in full control of the business logic in your applications. This control is often a source of inefficiency. Think about the various on-ramps of existing applications you currently provide to your customers. Typically, these require you to maintain some sort of common API on your customers' behalf that they integrate with. Your customers are completely reliant on you for that service, so when it goes down, it causes issues for them.

A blockchain application shifts the burden away from you to the network. Customers can run and maintain their own nodes to integrate with the decentralised application, reducing the operating costs you face in providing the application. The business logic may also exist on the decentralised application (provided it is not commercially sensitive). This shifts what would have historically been run behind closed doors on an internal service to being readily accessible on the blockchain.

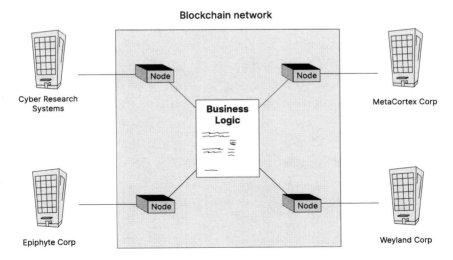

Business logic residing on a blockchain network

It is vital that you understand the implications of this contextual shift well in order to design your application appropriately.

CASE STUDY: A BLOCKCHAIN ISN'T A REGULAR DATABASE

Getting the balance right between what information resides on a blockchain or DLT isn't always easy, especially when customers are first working with the blockchain and fall into the trap of treating it like another storage technology.

We've seen this happen with a number of our clients: a blockchain platform has evolved and starts to store superfluous data similar to what would typically be stored in a traditional database, and hence users start to use it as a distributed database rather than a blockchain, with relationships between mutable entities.

Fortunately, our clients tend to be open-minded about what they're trying to do, and we've been able to re-educate them on how they should be thinking about using the ledger. This generally entails ensuring that the ledger is being used to record events, where these events represent transitions in state that are governed by rules encoded in smart contracts. These smart contracts apply business logic that consumes some input state and produces an output state on the ledger.

A minimum viable product

Having established a general architecture for your application or platform, it's now time to start building it out. We encourage our clients to think in terms of building a minimum viable product (MVP) adhering to an agile delivery methodology with ongoing input and feedback from potential customers.

Regardless of the size of your organisation or established processes you have in place, following a more cumbersome methodology will probably create additional burdens on the team that impact overall project delivery. You're trying to deliver something that is unlike any platform or application that's been done previously, so it's almost certain that your existing policies and procedures will need to be adapted to support the application delivery. You don't want to put a square peg into a round hole.

MVP versus PoC

It's important to draw out the distinction between an MVP versus a PoC, which we undertook in the previous phase. Creating an MVP[55] entails building out a minimalist version of your product or application that can demonstrate its core functionality and value to your clients or customers. Unlike a PoC, it is a fully working solution, but delivered in a minimalist manner.

The intent here is to be able to validate as early as possible that what you are building is what your customers or users want, rather than going down the path of creating a shiny complete product that doesn't meet their needs.

Delivery methodology

The delivery methodology that you use to support the MVP is also important. An agile approach will ensure that you are regularly demonstrating what is being built to stakeholders and customers and you are able to incorporate feedback or changes easily. This is due to the incremental and iterative nature of these types of delivery methodologies.

During the past decade, agile delivery methods were popularised by the Scrum framework for developing and sustaining solutions for applications. However, this still requires a significant number of meetings among various teams and stakeholders that need to be managed carefully to ensure there is adequate time available for the technical teams to perform their delivery.

While a detailed treatise of the most appropriate methodology is outside the scope of this book, I encourage you to explore more minimal delivery methodologies such as Kanban and Lean, given the greater uncertainty you will initially face with the delivery of your new application or platform.

In recent years, the Scaled Agile methodology[56] has gained traction in enterprise. It provides a framework based on the Scrum and the Lean methodologies, supporting teams, large programs and portfolio-size technical delivery. As with all frameworks, it's not perfect and needs to be adapted to suit your organisation, but parts of it could probably benefit your organisation if not already in use.

Remember – the underlying goal is to have something which provides you with feedback from real customers as early as possible. Being able to support this goal is more important than the nuances of the delivery approach you take.

CASE STUDY: THE IOT OPPORTUNITY

As one of the largest telecommunications companies in the world, Vodafone takes innovation very seriously, having been working on a number of blockchain-specific initiatives since 2017. Its goal is to create real business value and improve the customer experience with this technology.

In focusing on decentralised identity technology, Vodafone will be able to provide customers with greater control over their personal data while also simplifying access to its services. In addition, the resiliency of blockchain networks will help ensure that the single points of failure that have plagued many an enterprise's identity management services will be a thing of the past.

Vodafone is also heavily invested in Internet of Things (IoT) technology, providing SIM cards and the communication networks that allow them to communicate with one another and the cloud platforms that support them. Vodafone is building out its Digital Asset Broker platform using blockchain technology to allow IoT devices to transact directly with peer-to-peer services.

Both of these are areas where Web3 Labs has been actively collaborating with Vodafone on the architectural design and delivery of projects to support these strategically important services.

Go-to-market strategy

While the MVP is being built out, you'll want to start figuring out your full product launch. As you've been working with customers during this phase, you should be confident that what you are building addresses the problem you set out to solve.

The key consideration here is thinking about how you launch your product or platform to the wider market. It doesn't have to be a big-bang event, it may just be that you start to onboard more customers. The important thing is that you have a plan in place for how you will grow your customer and user base.

A wealth of information is already available on creating your go-to-market strategy.[57] However, when you're working with blockchain applications there are a few important additional considerations you need to be aware of; we refer to these as the GIS lifecycle – governance, interoperability and security.

The GIS lifecycle

It is vital that you factor in governance, interoperability and security considerations not just for your launch; you should also review them on an ongoing basis throughout the lifetime of your application.

They apply equally whether you are launching on a private or public blockchain. If you are currently running on a private network, however, you should be thinking about how in the longer term you can transition across or at the very least connect into a public blockchain network. Projects such as the Baseline Protocol, which we mentioned earlier, are geared toward running enterprise applications on top of public blockchain network infrastructure. This will be a significant area of growth during the coming years.

Governance

Governance in the context of blockchain platforms refers to how one approaches the management of the network among its participants. It includes considerations such as:

- The roles and responsibilities of node operators

- How changes or modifications to the network are proposed and managed, potentially using a decentralised approach to governance as we discussed in Part One

- The network upgrade process

- Participant onboarding

- How consensus is reached across the network

When working with a private, permissioned blockchain network, your organisation and the other organisations in the network need to reach agreement on how to approach governance. Given the complexities dealing with just one external organisation, when you extrapolate this out to dealing with a network of external organisations, you can quickly appreciate how much more complex this can get, which is why you need to have clearly defined rules and responsibilities for participants to adhere to.

When working with a public blockchain network, the governance is less complex on the surface, as you are simply establishing connectivity to a network that has its own governance model established. However, it is vital that you appreciate that governance model; its approach will dictate how that network evolves over time. Hence you will need to ensure your organisation is comfortable with keeping on top of the upgrades to support changes as they happen.

Keep in mind, too, that it's unlikely you will be able to exert significant influence on governance decisions due to the sheer number of participants on public networks.

Type of network	Advantages	Disadvantages
Private blockchain	Ability to directly influence governance and control pace of change.	Complex onboarding. Dependencies on other organisations in network, which may have differing business models or priorities, or operate with different jurisdictional constraints.
Public blockchain	Simpler onboarding, usually opaque governance.	Inability to significantly influence governance.

Given these considerations, you need to have clarity on your governance model and have support from potential node operators (if using a private-permissioned network), before you perform your wider launch.

Managed blockchain services

One approach that can help reduce the overhead of governance is to partner with a company that provides managed blockchain networks services,[58] as they can run blockchain networks on behalf of organisations. However, you need to ensure that the infrastructure they provide can be spread across the network members' individual infrastructures, otherwise you are simply centralising the blockchain infrastructure with the provider, which defeats the purpose.

The provider may offer tools that streamline the operator experience. However, it must not be using its own proprietary approach here – you need to avoid vendor lock-in and it should be straightforward to migrate off their service down the line, should you wish to.

Interoperability

The United Nations Statistics division provides a useful framework[59] for thinking about the different types of interoperability that exist across systems.

Layer	Description	Example
Technology	Common interfaces that support interoperability at the technical layer	Blockchain or cross-ledger interoperability
Data	Common data formats and metadata	Smart contract languages
Human	Shared vocabularies and understanding of data	Documentation and agreements between partners
Institutional	Legal agreements between organisations such as licences and data-sharing agreements	Formalised governance process

With this framework, we can see how the governance process should help support interoperability from the institutional perspective.

In building out your PoC and MVP, you will have probably focused on the data and human layers. You will also have thought about how you can get your regular applications to talk to the blockchain applications. However, you may not have started to think about interoperability at the blockchain layer, simply because you're working with a single blockchain technology initially.

The number of blockchain platforms to choose from is ever-increasing; there isn't going to be one blockchain to rule them all, as much as some of the blockchain maximalists on Twitter would have you believe. There are a number of different platforms to choose from currently, some of which I list in the Resources section of this book. What this means from a practical perspective is that it's likely down the line that you will need to interoperate with other blockchains that exist, regardless of whether you are working with a public or private blockchain.

Interoperability is a moving target at present, with significant research and development activities taking place on an ongoing basis. The most common types of blockchain interoperability include:

- Token: Transferring a cryptocurrency or token between blockchains

- State: The transfer of a smart contract or decentralised application's state from one blockchain to another

- Oracles: Services that transfer external data to a blockchain, such as the price of a financial instrument

The landscape is constantly evolving, with the ultimate goal of achieving atomic transfers, whereby a singular transaction can be initiated to move the asset or state from one blockchain to another.

Although unlikely to impact your launch, you should think about at what point interoperability becomes relevant for your application. If you are starting out with a private, permissioned blockchain, you may want to test the waters and have some information from this network go to a public network. Or perhaps some of what you're creating or tracking on the private network should ultimately exist on a publicly accessible network. An example here would be any consumer-focused token – if it exists on a public network, the users gain greater utility with it.

You may be facing existing organisational barriers to integrating with a public network, but as the technology matures, in the same way that organisations are comfortable with having public presences on the internet and using internet services such as cloud providers, that level of comfort and safety will exist for blockchain.

If you are working with a public blockchain network already, you may find that other ecosystems or platforms exist on other blockchain networks that you'd like to integrate with. Again, how to do this interoperability is a key consideration. There are blockchains in the public domain that are dedicated to interoperability and that provide gateways for this purpose; however, this is not yet as seamless as it will be.

They key takeaway here is not that you have to start embracing interoperability technology on day one, but that you're aware of how it can assist you in benefiting from the broader innovations happening across blockchain networks.

CASE STUDY: PUBLIC BLOCKCHAIN INTEROPERABILITY

The opportunities for blockchain platforms providing interoperability are vast given the proliferation of different, available blockchain networks. One such platform is ICON, which is a public blockchain network for decentralised applications.[60] It is an aggregator network in that it provides interoperability across multiple blockchain networks referred to as communities.

We worked with the ICON Foundation on its Blockchain Transmission Protocol (BTP). BTP is its core blockchain interoperability framework; it provides cryptocurrency and token transfers between blockchain networks. Given the number of different public blockchain protocols that are available, one of the challenges ICON faces is how it can not only technically deliver such a protocol, but also integrate with more protocols than any other interoperability network. Web3 Labs started working with the ICON Foundation on addressing both of these challenges.

Our deep expertise in blockchain protocol development ensured that we were able to both drive the core protocol implementation and provide the plumbing to talk to leading blockchain networks, including Binance's Smart Chain platform.

The end result is that users of ICON have the ability to safely transfer tokens from one public blockchain network to another, which is non-trivial given how much value is at stake on these public blockchain networks.

Security

In some respects, the security considerations associated with blockchain networks are very familiar, such as the management of the cryptographic keys that underpin them. There are well-established technologies and services to support these.

However, you'll need to keep a couple of important topics front of mind in the design stage:

1. Wallet or key management
2. Managing network connectivity

It is possible that your organisation will not be familiar with how to approach these items from a security perspective, so it's important that you engage information security teams early on to obtain their buy-in with what you're trying to achieve.

Wallet management and custody

We discussed in Part One how cryptocurrency wallets are used in the storage of digital assets. These wallets contain a cryptographic key. In many public blockchain networks, cryptocurrency wallets are a form of identity on the network, as they are used to initiate transactions such as transferring a crypto asset from one person to another, or invoke some functionality on a smart contract.

If your organisation is using a public blockchain network, you will need to take custody of and manage the crypto assets associated with the wallet – or find a suitable provider to be custodian and manager on your behalf. This is another reason why organisations are less keen on working with public blockchains initially, as dealing with cryptocurrencies will likely require various approvals because it could be determined to be another type of asset held on your balance sheet (even if in small amounts).

Of course, if your organisation is planning to create a new entity or raise funds via some sort of token sale, then having custody solutions in place will be of paramount importance to you.

Cryptocurrency wallets also provide a degree of anonymity for users, which is not what businesses want. Businesses need to know exactly who they are dealing with, whether they are complying with KYC or antimoney laundering (AML) regulations, or simply that who they are dealing with is who they believe they are.

Thus wallets ideally need to be linked to some form of identity, be it tied to an individual, department, business unit or organisation. Solutions exist to address this shortcoming: tying blockchain accounts or wallets to verified individuals or organisations.

This can be achieved with decentralised identity solutions, but many enterprise-focused blockchain technologies build on top of the internet's public key infrastructure (PKI). This uses certificates to represent organisations or individuals. This technology is widely used in SSL/TLS on websites to prove that the web address you are visiting via your browser is genuine. These certificates[61] have cryptographic keys associated with them, which is one of the reasons why they are adopted in this context.

Regardless of the specific approach to accounts mandated by the platform you are using, you need a robust strategy in place for managing these credentials. Fortunately, the underlying cryptographic keys are already widely used in organisations and online in the context of public key cryptography. Examples include the aforementioned PKI, along with protocols such as SSL/TLS for securing access to websites, SSH for secure access to servers and IPSec for secure communication in VPNs.

The good news is that your security and information security teams should already have best practices and policies in place for managing these types of cryptographic keys, and devices such as hardware security modules are already widely used in enterprises across the world for them. However, blockchain platforms may use abstractions that require a degree of education to familiarise oneself with them.[62]

Connectivity and security

You will need to work with your security teams to establish connectivity to the blockchain network you are working with. If you are using a public network, there will be parallels with the provision of existing internet services, as you are allowing connectivity with unknown external entities.

In a private network you will know which organisations you are working with. However, there is likely to be a large number of organisations with which to establish connectivity; this is a non-trivial change as far as security teams are concerned.

In addition, the protocols being used by the blockchain platform are unlikely to be familiar to your security teams, which they may take issue with initially as they will not able to easily monitor the traffic going in and out of your organisation. Hence, they may need to create bespoke proxy services on top of these blockchain nodes. Although many of the platforms targeting enterprises provide services to this end.

The smart contracts or code powering the decentralised applications may also benefit from audits by an external entity. For applications running on public blockchains that hold tokens or cryptocurrencies this is absolutely essential. The DAO hack we mentioned in Chapter 4 illustrates an extreme case of what can go wrong here. Even for private blockchains such an audit may be diligent, depending on what's at stake in the event of there being a bug in the decentralised application code.

Then there is the overall security of the system. Techniques such as penetration testing may be considered to simulate attacks from hackers. Unfortunately, the traditional approach to penetration testing is not adequate to fully verify the security of a blockchain network. You are not providing a service with well-defined integration points such as an API-based service, you are provisioning a blockchain network whose boundaries exceed your organisation's infrastructure. This means that while you can apply penetration testing techniques to ascertain the security of components of the network that you are responsible for, the decentralised nature of the network means that you cannot guarantee that same level of security throughout.

Hence, you need to follow closely all guidance issued by the provider of the blockchain service, and ensure you rigorously adhere to standard best practices such as:

- Keeping all software up to date

- Performing regular threat assessments

- Enforcing least privilege access

- Embracing automation

The differences that blockchain networks present with respect to both wallet or key management and connectivity considerations will require ongoing support from your security teams, so you must ensure they are aware of what you're trying to achieve and supportive of it before you move on to the next stage – deployment.

Summary

The goal of the design phase is to start building out an MVP of your solution.

To do this you will need to:

- Take on board learnings from the discovery phase

- Aim to have strategic support at the executive level

- Engage a small number of customers or end-users to work with you

- Share the vision of the platform with the technical teams to create alignment

Alongside the creation of the MVP, additional considerations include:

- Your go-to-market strategy and how you will launch the product

- The governance approach to managing the network

- How you will secure the network and cryptographic keys

- How you will address interoperability, if applicable

Avoid the mistake of treating a DLT or blockchain as a traditional data storage platform.

10
Deploy

The deployment phase is where we take all of the preparation we performed during the design phase and bring our decentralised application to market.

Although the best laid plans often go awry, you should be confident by this phase that you have:

- A minimum viable product you can launch

- A comprehensive go-to-market strategy to follow

- Engagement from key stakeholders and customers

- Established your approach to governance

- Identified any interoperability requirements

- Buy-in from security teams and established security practices to support the deployment

This will ensure you are as well prepared as you can be for your launch.

The type of launch

In building your MVP, you should have been working with a select group of customers to ensure that what you've built addresses their specific pain points. The outcome is to now go live with the MVP in a production environment setting, and you can approach this in two ways – as either a soft or a hard go-live.

A hard go-live requires opening up your application to all of your potential customers at once. If you are releasing a fully decentralised application on a public blockchain it will be available to anyone with an internet connection. That said, the biggest challenge for most products and services is building their user base, so unless you have generated a significant buzz about your new blockchain-based product or service via your go-to-market strategy and effective use of social media channels, or you have an existing customer base that you are opening the platform up to at once, this is unlikely to be too significant an issue.

Typically, the only time you should have to perform a hard go-live, where you are forced to make your platform available to as many customers as possible, is when external

pressures force your hand, such as regulatory requirements. Given the emerging nature of blockchain technology, this may not be an issue for the next few years.
Even if you are facing significant competitor pressures, I
would encourage you not to go down this route, unless
there really is no other option.

A soft go-live takes a phased approach to opening up and
bringing new customers on board with your platform.
As you will have worked with some initial customers
in building out the MVP, you should have some willing
participants to work with you at this stage. They will
be familiar with the work, which you should have validated addresses a real need they have, so they should be
supportive of working with you.

Once you go live with the new platform with this first
batch of customers, you will undertake subsequent phases
where you onboard further batches of customers to the
platform.

Customer onboarding

Depending on the type of blockchain you are working
with, public or private, you will need to address
onboarding considerations to support your customers.

In the case of a private-permissioned blockchain, you are
likely to need to support two types of customers – those

who want to be active network participants and those who don't.

The active network participants not only want to make use of the product or service that the platform provides, but also be involved in the governance of the network and run their own network infrastructure, which they typically use to interact with the network. Exactly how they run this infrastructure is down to their own individual preference – they may engage a separate provider to achieve this on their infrastructure, as we discussed in the governance section of the last chapter. The key thing is that they want to access the network via a decentralised infrastructure they manage themselves or through a provider. This approach requires ongoing management of the blockchain node software and physical connectivity between other participants.

Inactive network participants are those that do not want the overhead of running any blockchain network infrastructure; they simply want a gateway they can use to access the decentralised application. In a private blockchain setting, this access is often provided via another network participant and is distinct from active participants using a third-party service.

In a public blockchain application, customers may still wish to be active network participants and run their own network infrastructure. However, given the public nature of these networks, the manner in which they go about this will be aligned with best practices as per that network, rather than your application. You can advise participants of potential approaches they can use here, such as how they go about running their own blockchain node on the network.

If they want to be inactive participants in a public network, you can recommend API-based service providers that can provide access.

There is more flexibility with a public network, as the public blockchain platform is distinct from your application and less tightly coupled than it is likely to be with a private network.

The table below sums up the considerations for the types of participants.

	Public blockchain	Private blockchain
Active participant	Run and maintain blockchain node software with open connectivity to network	Run and maintain blockchain node software with point-to-point connections to all participants
Inactive participant	Access via third-party API service	Delegated access via another network participant

Training

In both the onboarding of new customers and transitioning your application to a live environment, you will need to provide adequate training to ensure that both the customers using and the teams managing your application are comfortable working with it.

We already discussed the need to work with security teams to highlight the differences decentralised platforms present. It is no different with customers and support teams, who will need to appreciate how decentralised applications are different.

Customers will need to have at least some awareness of how blockchain technology is being used behind the scenes. It may be necessary to demonstrate how to work with some of the blockchain wallet technologies, depending on the functionality the application provides. For instance, if users are presented with a mobile or web application they may have a wallet on their device that is used to invoke or approve transactions.

Additionally, if their organisation is an active participant in the network, their infrastructure teams will need to undergo similar training to those managing your application within your organisation.

Similarly, the teams managing your applications will need to gain familiarity with the underlying blockchain platform you are using. To assist them with this, it is important that they can establish good working relationships with both the vendors of the blockchain platform and the teams responsible for delivering the blockchain components of your application, such as the developers working on the smart contracts or equivalent.

If there is no vendor providing the blockchain platform, for instance if a free, open-source application is being used, the team responsible for deploying and managing the platform would be your best port of call for platform support.

Support

The decentralised nature of the platform means that it won't always be obvious when issues emerge what has caused them. It's important that you have created good documentation for your platform that provides steps to assist troubleshooting and gives answers to frequently answered questions. It amazes me how often technical projects overlook quality documentation; in the public domain it can make or break open-source projects, but this mindset isn't always carried through to internal initiatives.

The next port of call should be the technical teams with responsibility for the overall application. They will be best placed to deal with arising issues and figure out if it is down to a bug in their code or something strange happening at the blockchain layer.

Appropriate monitoring and analytics tools should be deployed to help provide greater visibility of the overall health of the platform at an operational level. There are blockchain-specific tools that exist for exactly this purpose.

CASE STUDY: MONITORING DIGITAL BONDS

At Web3 Labs we created the Epirus Blockchain Explorer specifically for providing monitoring and visualisation of blockchain networks. One of our customers is BOOSTRY Co. Ltd, a joint venture company established by Nomura Holdings, Inc. and Nomura Research Institute, Ltd (NRI).

BOOSTRY provided the technical infrastructure to support NRI on its digital asset bond and digital bond offering. This was a significant event as it was the first bond offering by a Japanese issuer using blockchain technology.

Shunsuke Hagihira, infrastructure engineer at BOOSTRY Co., and his team understood that being a new entrant to business in Japan can be extremely difficult due to the regulations in place and the arduous process of obtaining the correct trading licences.

To simplify the process, the BOOSTRY team created ibet, a consortium blockchain platform. ibet issues various rights and trading methods as security tokens, which are programmed by smart contracts on the blockchain. These security tokens represent digitalised securities such as stocks, bonds and real estate, but the team has ambitions to expand to corporate bonds, memberships and service usage rights.

With the ibet platform having such huge potential, it soon became clear to Shunsuke Hagihira that he needed a way to reliably monitor all transactions on the network.

BOOSTRY Co. first began to use Epirus Blockchain Explorer in December 2019 after identifying the need for a quick and easy way to monitor transactions on ibet.

By using our Epirus Blockchain Explorer, Shunsuke Hagihira found that he could quickly and easily monitor the ibet network. He was particularly impressed with the intelligent monitoring system on the dashboard as all of the key metrics were at his fingertips, such as breakdowns of transactions over various time windows and the business events coming from contracts on the network.

'Epirus [Blockchain Explorer] has provided BOOSTRY with the meaningful business intelligence and insights they needed to manage the rapid growth outlined in the joint ventures above. They have welcomed the great user experience and sophisticated functionality of the Epirus Blockchain Explorer that enables them to gain the information they need from their network in a quick and pain free way.'

Maintenance and release management

As we discussed in the section on security in the previous chapter, ongoing maintenance of the platform is crucial. In addition, you will constantly be evolving and adapting the application to address bugs and provide new features to your users.

The blockchain infrastructure can be patched and upgraded much like any standard services. However, unlike many traditional services such as databases, you wouldn't typically bring a blockchain platform offline to perform upgrades. Upgrades should take place on a node by node basis while the network remains available. (Remember the unstoppable machine from Chapter 1?)

The upgrade approach will vary depending on the underlying blockchain platform you are working with, and the decentralised applications running on top of the network. Due to the immutable nature of blockchains, you cannot update existing data. Hence, your upgrade path typically involves creating new versions of the decentralised application and pointing the other components or users of the system towards it.

Blockchain platforms have various approaches to managing decentralised applications; what we commonly see on smart contract-based platforms such as Ethereum is a proxy contract.[63] Proxy contracts are used to handle all requests for your application and route them to the latest version of the application code. This ensures that customers or services using the decentralised application always go via the same access point.

The documentation for the blockchain platform you are using should provide details of the best practices regarding release and upgrade management, as approaches can vary.

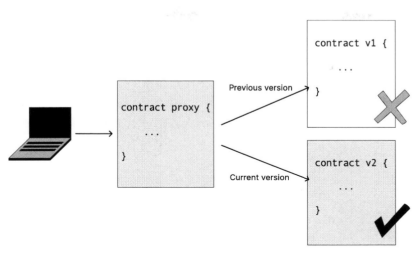

A smart contract proxy

Eliminate single points of failure

Although blockchain platforms themselves provide a high level of resiliency and availability when deployed correctly, it's vital not to overlook the potential for single points of failure that could impact the availability of the application. When you first launch your MVP to a select group of customers, you may have a level of goodwill you can tap into should an outage occur, but this isn't ideal. It's impossible to guarantee against outages, but important to proactively try to identify all single points of failure before they come back and bite you. As Murphy's Law states: 'Anything that can go wrong, will go wrong.'

Historically, we have seen time and time again centralised services falling over and bringing enterprises to their knees.

Sometimes it can be a seemingly insignificant event, such as a bad update to a domain name system (DNS) record bringing core services down and creating widespread outages, resulting in millions of dollars in lost revenue. In another instance, failures at data centres that expose weaknesses in business continuity planning can cause significant issues for the business.

The world's largest tech companies aren't immune to this either – Google, Facebook, Microsoft's Azure cloud and Amazon Web Services, to name a few, have all suffered major outages in the past few years.[64] Many of those services, such as cloud providers, have a trickle-down effect on the wider internet, bringing down popular sites such as Airbnb and Netflix in the process.

The resiliency of public blockchain networks such as Bitcoin and Ethereum[65] is incredibly impressive when compared with these large, but centralised services controlled by individual companies. Private blockchains, if configured correctly with a large enough number of participants, with the nodes spread sensibly geographically and on a variety of infrastructures, should also be able to exhibit similar resiliency.

However, just because the underlying blockchain is resilient, it doesn't mean your platform will be. If you're relying on an infrastructure provider to access that blockchain, what happens if that provider has an outage?[66] If you're hosting the blockchain nodes yourself, have you built adequate resiliency into them?

How about the so-called regular services that are built on top of the blockchain components? Are suitable resiliency patterns built into them? Do you have any data storage technologies that perform data extraction from the blockchain for activities such as caching or reporting? Is there adequate redundancy there? The list goes on.

When assessing the platform's security considerations, if you performed activities such as a threat assessment, combined with identifying and addressing potential weaknesses in the application architecture or infrastructure, you should be in a far better position to maintain resiliency and uptime of your decentralised application.

Legal considerations

Depending on the industry that your organisation operates in and the scale of the problem or opportunity that you're trying to address, it's likely you will need to resolve legal considerations. It's not uncommon in significant blockchain projects that the legal or regulatory hurdles that need to be overcome are bigger than the technology challenges you face, and have to be costed for accordingly.

As my background is in the technology profession rather than legal, none of what I say next should be considered legal advice, but hopefully it can be used to trigger conversations with the appropriate people.

The types of challenges you may have to consider include:

- The types of data that you are storing, especially as it is likely sensitive

- Where the data is being stored – some financial regulators dictate where transactional data must physically reside

- The format in which it is stored – these days data should be stored in an encrypted form during transit and at rest

- Are the activities performed by smart contracts legally enforceable, and what if they fail? An example would be if you have a smart contract representing a bill of lading or payments on a bond coupon

- Duration and retention of data

- Ability and speed of access to data – often there are requirements in the financial services industry to be able to produce data within short periods of notice if so required by a regulator

- How data held on an immutable blockchain sits with legal rights, such as the right to be forgotten

As blockchains can span geographic borders and organisations, and legal arrangements between organisations take time to establish, addressing legal considerations could end up being one of the most time-consuming aspects of the deployment. This can be especially challenging if you are working with a public blockchain on which you cannot restrict activity in specific jurisdictions. Hence, you need to pull in your legal counsel early to ensure you don't hit any significant barriers at launch.

What about GDPR?

The European Union's General Data Protection Regulation (GDPR), which came into effect in 2018, dictates that organisations holding data on individuals must take adequate measures to protect that data and use it only for lawful reasons specified in the regulation. One such reason concerns an organisation fulfilling its contractual obligations to an individual customer. Not only is the protection of customer data crucial, the legislation also dictates that the individual has the right at any time to revoke their consent to the organisation using their data.

The immutable nature of blockchains naturally does not lend itself to being an appropriate place to store any customer data, nor should it be treated as a distributed database as we discussed earlier. In addition, in a blockchain the same data is made available to all participants, which again isn't ideal.

That being said, you may have events related to customer activities you wish to record. Fortunately, blockchains provide additional privacy measures, such as data encryption and the exchange of information off the blockchain (off-chain) via secure channels. The specifics of this depend on the blockchain or DLT[67] you are working with.

Where next?

Given that no two organisations are the same, there is no one size fits all approach to getting the deployment phase right. If you follow the steps I've outlined you will minimise the likelihood of issues arising post go-live that could derail your project down the line.

By encompassing all the steps across the discovery, design and deployment phases, you can be confident that not only are you validating a viable use case for blockchain technology in your organisation, but also that the way in which you bring something live to real customers is built upon sustainable foundations. At this point, your application or platform should start to look more like the solution to the problem you set out to solve, and less the shiny new tool in the toolbox.

Summary

The deploy phase encompasses the go-live of your blockchain application or platform.

Considerations during this phase include:

- Whether to perform a soft or hard go-live when launching your application or platform. A hard go-live should only be necessary if there are regulatory or competitive pressures that force your hand

- How you onboard your customers – gradually is preferable

- Providing appropriate training for your customers and support teams

- Ensuring adequate support via quality documentation, support staff and appropriate monitoring and analytics tools

- The approaches to maintenance and release management

It may also be necessary to engage your legal counsel if there are regulatory constraints you need to adhere to.

PART THREE

MAKING IT HAPPEN

Now that you are clear on the approach to follow for blockchain-based digital transformations and many of the considerations that are unique to blockchain and DLT technology, it's important that you can perform the necessary steps to get an initiative off the ground.

In this final part of the book you will be armed with the resources to make this happen, and further context that will provide you with confidence in your approach.

11

Community And Collaboration

Significant communities have formed around block-chain and DLT technology, which manage to be both incredibly diverse and well aligned to service the needs of enterprise.

This is due to the perceived opportunity provided by this technology, which not only has the potential to affect many layers of society, but also significantly impact the world of business and bring great new efficiencies to the market.

In this chapter I'll be discussing what makes this community unique and the many areas for collaboration that exist in industry.

Unlearn what you know

We discussed earlier the importance of being able to challenge your existing thinking, addressing those biases that often prevent people from taking a fresh perspective on existing problems or challenges.

It's useful to re-emphasise the importance of doing this so you don't switch back to your default modes of thinking where it feels too difficult to look into this technology now, due to other more pressing or immediate concerns.

Those other items trying to capture your attention will always be there; there will never be a better time than now to embark on a new opportunity and, once you set off on the journey, there will be no looking back. Getting involved with the communities that have sprung up around blockchain is a great way to stay inspired and keep abreast of everything that's happening.

The blockchain community is unique

Once you start exploring everything that is taking place within the blockchain industry – spanning cryptocurrencies, enterprise blockchain, protocols, DAOs, DeFi and NFTs – you will find it's a far more interesting and fun place to be than many more traditional technology domains. The reason for this is simple – the breadth of people that blockchain technology impacts and provides opportunity for is incredible. At one extreme you have established enterprises finding ways to disintermediate their own industry practices, creating new market opportunities to provide value to existing and new customers. At the other extreme you have the crypto-rich who were lucky with their crypto investments, artists creating NFTs and radical libertarians who want to be free of traditional fiscal and monetary systems.

Hence you have innovations that are transcending industries, age, gender, income and culture. There's not a single demographic or geography that isn't touched by the transformative potential here, and you can experience this firsthand by attending blockchain community-focused conferences such as the Ethereum Foundation's annual DevCon conference.

This diversity of interests and mindset that blockchain serves means it is a truly unique place to be right now, and hence much more fun than more traditional emerging technology domains. It's a well-known fact that diverse companies are more profitable. The leading management consulting firm McKinsey's 2015 report on diversity in public companies stated that the top quartile of racially and ethnically diverse companies were 35% more likely to have better returns than their industry mean.[68]

The diversity within the blockchain industry means there is a far more interesting pool of talent out there to look to for inspiration, but also potentially to tap into for your own initiatives, which helps ensure you can have the right mix of people driving these, who you may not typically have access to.

CASE STUDY: FROM MINING CRYPTO TO WEB3J

My own initial foray into blockchain technology provided a great opportunity to see how diverse this community was compared with many other areas I'd been involved in previously.

It started with me building a cryptocurrency mining rig. The Ethereum network's original consensus mechanism relied on solving a difficult mathematical problem,[69] which graphics cards are very good at. So I decided to build a dedicated computer for mining ether, the cryptocurrency of the Ethereum network.

This project entailed finding ways to connect multiple graphics cards to a computer motherboard and build a metal case to house it. A standard computer case wouldn't work as the graphics cards would be generating a lot of heat while the rig was running. There were also power consumption considerations as I needed to ensure that my electricity supply could provide the requisite amount of power and that the cost of this made economic sense given the return in cryptocurrency I was obtaining.

Once the physical challenges were overcome, I had to understand how to run a node on the Ethereum network and manage the wallet in which funds were sent. From there I started discovering more about how one develops smart contracts, and the shortfalls there ultimately led me to develop the software library Web3j.[70]

In sharing my work with the Sydney Ethereum community (at the time I was residing in Australia), I started to meet other people passionate about the technology and its potential impact. This made me appreciate how different this community was compared with other technology communities I had been involved in previously.

This combination of challenges provided by the Ethereum blockchain was very different to those I experienced previously building computers and learning conventional programming languages. It sent me in a completely new direction and I've had a lot of fun in the process. This is why I encourage you to embrace the fun mindset with blockchain, as it really can take you to unexpected places.

Collaboration is key

Blockchain is by its nature a collaborative technology. You cannot have a public network running on top of the internet without high degrees of collaboration taking place between individuals as well as organisations.

This extends to private blockchain deployments too – organisations need to collaborate with one another to get a network off the ground. Existing consortia can be used, but more often than not, new consortia are established.

Regardless of which approach you take, you must be prepared to collaborate with other organisations to benefit from blockchain.

This sometimes presents a dilemma for companies that are used to viewing other organisations in their industry with a competitive mindset. The important thing here is to identify those win-win areas of the business that are not a primary source of your competitive advantage. You want to focus on those that are slow and inefficient and support the primary revenue-generating activities, but do not directly impact them.

Some widely cited examples include back- and middle-office functions within banks that settle and clear transactions, or those industries that still are passing physical documents between multiple organisations, such as bills of lading in the shipment of cargo across supply chains.

Blockchain can streamline these types of non-differentiating activities, which are widely recognised and criticised within these industries as weak links, often considered pain points for all, an ongoing source of inefficiency and a cost to businesses. In bringing different organisations together to address these problems you also benefit from a diversity of perspectives in how you solve them, as each organisation has its own unique view on the problem.

Collaboration via open-source software

The location where the actual code resides, to be collaborated on by technology teams for blockchain projects, is a consideration. The willingness to embrace open-source software varies from one organisation to another due to concerns around protecting their intellectual property.

However, platforms where code can easily be shared and contributed to by multiple organisations should be used.

In the public blockchain domain, most of the code supporting blockchain protocols resides on the open-source code collaboration platforms GitHub and, to a lesser extent, GitLab. The reason is that these platforms provide a neutral hosting location.

Private code repositories can be used to restrict access easily to consortia member organisations, so an appropriate level of IP protection can be enforced at the code level if desired.

Industry and standards groups

You may feel that the existing industry groups or consortia your organisation is plugged into are not aligned with your goals for blockchain, or perhaps you just want to get a better understanding of what other firms are doing. This is where blockchain-specific industry groups can be invaluable.

Many organisations have been created to help foster blockchain adoption in industry, some of which are creating standards to help support overall adoption, while others are focused on specific industry verticals. The table below summarises the types of organisation that exist, with examples of blockchain and those that are not focused on blockchain to provide additional context.

	Standards development organisations	Open source foundations	Industry standards organisations	Industry consortia
Focus	Technology innovation	Technology innovation	Market innovation	Market innovation
Goal	Creation of high-quality standards to support general industry adoption of new technology	Hosting of open-source software projects	Creation of standards and product certifications for specific industries. Forums for discussion and education initiatives.	Establish industry consortia focusing on specific use cases
Examples	• Institute of Electrical and Electronic Engineers • Enterprise Ethereum Alliance	• Apache Software Foundation • Hyperledger	• Internet Engineering Taskforce • ETSI • Global Blockchain Business Council • MOBI • Decentralised Identity Foundation • EU Blockchain Observatory and Forum	• World Wide Web Consortium (W3C) • IBM Food Trust • Onyx by J.P. Morgan

Adapted from Ramesh Ramadoss, 'The Role of the IWA in the Standardization Landscape'[71]

Referring to the membership lists of these industry organisations can serve as a useful starting point in deciding which organisations to join. Keep in mind that unless you just want to use your membership for PR purposes, you are required to make a time commitment to get the most value from these organisations. You want to have at least one, ideally a few individuals to represent your interests and contribute to relevant initiatives to get the most out of them.

The type of contributions could include:

- Contributing to standards efforts via the editorial process or making individual contributions

- Presenting at working group meetings on relevant initiatives your organisation is involved in

The great thing about these bodies is that if a specific focus area or working group doesn't exist that serves the needs of your business, you can create one (provided it is aligned with the broader goals of the industry or standards group), creating a spotlight that your organisation can use to drive greater awareness of work relevant to your organisation.

CASE STUDY: CREATING INDUSTRY STANDARDS

During the past four years, I have taken an active role in the creation of industry standards to help increase blockchain adoption, starting with the Enterprise

Ethereum Alliance and, more recently, the InterWork Alliance, a Global Blockchain Business Council initiative.

The Enterprise Ethereum Alliance was launched in March 2017 with the goal of driving industry adoption of Ethereum technology via collaboration and the establishing of industry standards suitable for enterprise.

In August 2017 I took on the role of chair of the Technical Specification Working Group, which focused on creating an Enterprise Ethereum client specification. The word client is used in this context to refer to the software that the nodes making up the Ethereum network run. Running the software makes a computer a client of the network.

One of the challenges faced by enterprises that had chosen to work with Ethereum technology was that multiple vendors were building client technology that provided additional privacy, permissioning and performance features on top of standard Ethereum software, but they did not go about it in a standardised manner. To avoid vendor lock-in, an industry standard needed to be created to support this.

In conjunction with contributions from member firms, following best practices adopted by industry standards bodies like the World Wide Web Consortium (W3C), I created the Enterprise Ethereum architecture stack and oversaw the creation and publication of the world's first Enterprise Ethereum client specification.[72]

The powerful thing about going through this process is that you get a level of engagement from representatives across a wide number of organisations, whether small or large, for profit or not for profit. This enables you to understand the different goals and perspectives that these parties have for this technology, as well as appreciate the variety of differing viewpoints that need to be catered for in the creation of specifications. This process provides confidence that what is being produced is generally fit for purpose, which is a degree of understanding you simply couldn't obtain from working within a silo in a singular organisation.

Consortia caveats

You may find that joining or establishing a consortium is more appropriate for your organisation. Existing consortia can provide the necessary infrastructure and platform for you to work with, reducing the overall heavy lifting required from a technology perspective. You will need to jump through a number of legal hoops, but hopefully the organisation or foundation running the consortium can provide this for you.

If you are establishing the consortium yourself, you will need to find a way to get all the legal frameworks and technology in place between members, some of which we touched on in the previous chapter.

Unlike the other types of industry group, a consortium may be set up as for-profit as well as non-profit. This can lead to additional considerations around areas such as intellectual property and antitrust claims due to the potential for collision among member firms.

Much like traditional consortia, commercial blockchain consortia are often spun up as joint ventures between the founding firms, creating a dedicated entity to build and support it.[73]

Summary

The diversity of its community provides blockchain with a unique opportunity, because of its potential impact across society.

The collaborative nature of blockchain extends beyond the individual to businesses working together to establish large blockchain consortia in order to address some of the big challenges impacting their industry.

Open-source software provides the basis for collaboration at the technical level, while conferences, industry and standards groups provide platforms for collaboration spanning individuals as well as organisations.

Relevant blockchain industry groups include:

- Decentralised Identity Foundation

- The Enterprise Ethereum Alliance

- Hyperledger

- The Global Blockchain Business Council

Established blockchain conferences include:

- CoinDesk's Consensus
- The Ethereum Foundation's DevCon
- Hyperledger Global Forum

12

Innovation And Risk

There's never going to be a perfect time to strike out on a new, innovative initiative, just like no one can consistently call the top of the market. For every big success there are hundreds, potentially thousands, of failures and, while we want to minimise risk, it's important to acknowledge that these failures provide the key opportunities for subsequent learning, which is the foundation for innovation.

As long as these learnings are shared, valuable assets are being generated in the form of knowledge within your organisation. Regardless of what your competitors are doing, it's important you have an innovator's mindset and approach innovation with the right attitude, which is what I'm going to discuss in this chapter.

An innovation dilemma

Clayton Christensen argued in his seminal book, *The Innovator's Dilemma*,[74] that incumbent firms don't prioritise innovation as it is perceived as complex due to the uncertainty of the tangible benefits it will provide. This leads to a classic trap – these firms get disrupted by new entrants who have found ways to create new types of products, embracing the architectural paradigm provided by new technology.

Some of the more forward-thinking incumbents try to apply this new type of innovation to their existing business, but inevitably it doesn't provide direct value to their existing products or services, thus their experimentation ends. Others simply are not willing to risk harming existing healthy product or service margins with products that could disrupt their own businesses.

Of course, you don't want to fall into these traps and, as you've read this far, you're unlikely to if you take heed of the above.

We discussed in Chapter 7 how you need to embrace new paradigms in how you view your organisation by turning it inside out. You need to be aware of what's being built across the various blockchain ecosystems. This mindset will ensure that you don't make the mistake of treating a blockchain platform as just another storage technology. This is an error we see time and time again, where businesses treat blockchains or DLTs much like databases, and put far too much data on the ledger. Rather than looking to existing, established architectural practices within your company, you should be studying how the vendors of ledger technologies are structuring their public libraries and frameworks, or examining the smart contracts of popular public blockchain protocols and projects themselves.

I reiterate, given the importance of this – please do not make the mistake of trying to replicate existing application or architectural paradigms onto a blockchain or DLT.

For those organisations that simply are not willing to risk disrupting their own business, there is a plethora of high-profile examples where this strategy fails. Think what you may about Tesla, it's hard to ignore its meteoric rise to being the most valuable car manufacturer with a market capitalisation that surpasses that of Toyota, Volkswagen, Daimler, GM, BMW, Honda, Hyundai, Fiat Chrysler and Ford[75] combined. All those companies dragged their feet and delayed investing heavily in electric vehicles. Back in 1996, General Motors released the EV1, which was the first mass-produced electric vehicle. Although the EV1 was popular with customers, General Motors believed electric vehicles were an unprofitable niche of the car market and ultimately scrapped most of the cars.[76] Had they defined success criteria in terms of creating something their customers actually wanted and shared this insight internally, allowing it to build internal momentum, it likely would have resulted in a very different outlook, with the initiative not crushed by senior management who were mistakenly focusing on standard internal and industry metrics.

Equally, a number of high-profile companies have managed to embrace this disruptive mindset. Look at how Microsoft managed to embrace the migration to cloud computing and open-source software, even though its core business had traditionally been in selling licences for its proprietary operating systems and productivity applications for on-premise servers and computers. Microsoft was being disrupted by cloud computing and free, browser-based versions of its core software offerings. It didn't just manage to adapt as an organisation; under Satya Nadella's leadership it's stronger than it's ever been with a market capitalisation of almost $2 trillion and diverse revenue streams across cloud computing, software licences, gaming and its own Surface computers.

Career risks

It's natural to shy away from taking risks if you are concerned it could impact your career. After all, who wants to be the person associated with the high-profile failure that cost the organisation millions of dollars that could have been used far more productively elsewhere? On the flip side, of course, if you're the person associated with a highly successful project, that will pay significant dividends for your career.

To address the downside risk concern – as the loss-aversion principle tells us, a loss is always far more painful than an equivalent gain – you need to ensure that there is a culture that is supportive of placing innovative bets. After all, that is what they are – you're rolling the dice to see if a prospective idea or innovation can provide the expected payoff. If it doesn't there's a cost, but there was never any guarantee of success at the outset. But that's OK as long as the right culture exists in your organisation to support this.

If it doesn't, and you feel genuinely stuck on how you can present a valid case, I encourage you to keep reading, as we cover how to go about this in a subsequent chapter. But in the worst case scenario, if you're reading a book on innovation and feel that you have no chance of being able to get the support you need to drive the change you believe is necessary, perhaps you should be looking elsewhere to an organisation that is willing to invest in an innovation strategy. After all, there's nothing worse than being stuck somewhere that doesn't value your leadership.[77]

CASE STUDY: ALMOST 200 YEARS OF INNOVATION

If you're concerned that your business or industry is too conservative or risk-averse in embracing innovative technologies, I encourage you to look to one of our customers, the insurance company Wakam (formerly La Parisienne), which was established in 1829.

Wakam recognises how important it is to continually innovate to maintain its leading market position. It has helped pioneer a new type of insurance platform – Insurance Product as a Service (IPaaS) – to automate claim management.

Henri Lieutaud, Lead Blockchain Developer at Wakam, described how 'blockchain technology was pivotal in developing IPaaS, as it provides a single source of truth for insurance and claims data, facilitating efficient money transfer between the parties involved in creating, underwriting and making claims on insurance products.'

Once Wakam had migrated all its insurance contracts for the IPaaS service, the challenge it then faced was how to make its data accessible and easy to track. The company had to ensure that it could query the data in a business-centric rather than a blockchain-centric manner. Using our Epirus Blockchain Explorer, the company was able to quickly and easily query the data and achieve a higher level of data organisation with the blockchain component of its platform.

'Epirus Blockchain Explorer is key for us, it helps us to get to a higher level of data organisation.'

The platform had to scale rapidly. Just two months after importing the initial 60,000 smart contracts to the blockchain, it rose to over 100,000 contracts. Now, the company has over 600,000 insurance policies on the platform, which is over 10% of all of their policies! Lieutaud has been amazed with this result and regards Epirus Blockchain Explorer as an integral factor that enabled the company to successfully meet the demands presented by such rapid growth.

'Because of the way the data is organised and the technology that is used, Epirus Explorer makes it easier to make a rest API call rather than to make an RPC [remote procedure call] request. We saved time as we did not have to develop anything ourselves and Web3 Labs' customer support quickly solved any issues we had. They also based new features on the feedback we gave them in order to meet our needs.'

Managing the downside

The question of how you can ensure you mitigate the downside risk of these innovative bets is vital. It's important to have a methodology in place that ensures you don't get ahead of yourself and take incremental steps with your exploration and subsequent build-out of a new platform or service. This is why I laid out the three-stage approach earlier, to ensure that you have a method to determine how much resource is required as you innovate with blockchain.

As you move further through the discovery, design and deploy process, it requires an ever-increasing investment on the part of your organisation. You progress by validating the assumptions that have taken you thus far and, ultimately, if it isn't right to continue on the path you're on, there's a way out. You're not trying to obtain the budget for a full deployment when you're only at the discovery phase, hence you have the ability to contain the downside risk of the investment to a level that you and the other various stakeholders can be comfortable with.

Summary

A balance needs to be struck between investing in your existing products and services versus innovation initiatives.

Companies that do not prioritise innovation often get disrupted in the long term by new entrants who have found ways to create new types of products. Tesla and Microsoft are two widely cited examples of companies that have managed to:

- Disrupt the market, in the case of Tesla

- Disrupt themselves, in the case of Microsoft

For innovation initiatives to succeed, your organisation should be supportive and have the appropriate controls in place so that they can be viewed as calculated bets rather than financial liabilities or risks.

13
Agility

The only constant in life is change, and blockchain and DLT are evolving rapidly. Being able to appreciate this and know how to respond are important considerations to ensure your business rides the wave (and doesn't get left behind) of wider industry disruption.

We are now going to delve further into the universal appeal of blockchain and articulate just how fast it is evolving.

Blockchain is a universal language

Imagine if the language barrier wasn't an issue in business. If, when you spoke to another company about integrating a new service between your businesses, there was zero ambiguity as to what the intent of this service was and how it was designed. That would be nice, right?

This notion of a common language that can bridge the boundaries of organisations and provides trust is one of the key concepts behind blockchain that we've discussed so far. However, I want you to think more about what this can do from a simplification perspective when it comes to defining the language used to describe transactions or events that take place, spanning your own business and others.

A number of industry protocols have been developed over the years to facilitate the transfer of information between businesses. In the financial industry the FIX protocol and FpML are two such examples. In other industries, you have the X12 Electronic Data Interchange format and eXtensible Business Reporting Language (XBRL) for exchanging business information.

These protocols provide messaging formats that support the exchange of information from one point to another, but the challenge still remains that the organisation on either side of the exchange has its own internal state that is updated on the back of this.

Blockchain and DLT networks enable us to take the internal state associated with these business transactions and move it outside the boundaries of our organisations into a shared place that is accessible to those who need it. Because these distributed networks provide a standardised protocol or API to work with them, it significantly simplifies how organisations can communicate with each other in a manner that both sides understand equally, thus removing one of the significant barriers that typically exist between organisations when communicating with one another.

This paradigm is incredibly powerful for thinking about what's possible, as it provides the same benefits of having a shared service provided by an external party, but without the overhead of having to work with niche communications protocols and a lack of information transparency between the provider and users of the service. Again, this is down to the decentralised nature and common API provided by blockchains.

The common layer also accelerates the rate at which solutions can be created that span these organisational boundaries, increasing the innovation opportunity for all.

Welcome to the Wild West

Regulation has a habit of playing catch-up with most innovation. Right now we're in the Wild West of cryptocurrency, with frontier towns being established in the form of new blockchain protocols and projects building on top of them.

This rate of change won't go on forever; to protect consumers, regulation will emerge that slows down the rate at which entities can innovate in this world. There will be significant penalties for organisations that choose not to play by the rules, with the goal of providing a safety net and additional layer of trust for those who may not be as savvy with the technology.

If we're lucky there will also be updates to existing regulations that can often seem archaic due to the fact that many of them predate any technological innovation. A classic example is the Howey Test, established under the Securities Act of 1933, which is used to determine if transactions qualify as investment contracts, which if they do are classified as securities and subject to regulatory requirements.

While the exact form of this regulation is unknown, when it does appear it will likely impact the overall rate of innovation taking place in the public blockchain landscape, affecting cryptocurrencies, tokens, stablecoins, NFTs and DeFi.

Interestingly, not all innovations have evolved in this manner. We've seen Facebook, Google, Amazon and other big tech firms able to grow in a somewhat unconstrained manner, with regulatory scrutiny starting to emerge only recently.

Tim Wu argued a decade ago[78] how every modern communications technology – the telephone, radio, cinema and TV – has eventually succumbed to the controlling embrace of government and corporations. In some instances, this regulation blocked major industries from emerging for a number of years. The Federal Communications Commission halted the evolution of television, just like it did previously with FM radio to prevent it upsetting the AM radio market.

Regardless at what point the regulatory landscape is established for industries, it not only hampers innovation, but also makes or breaks companies.

Larger, more established companies that have managed to establish a profitable business model fuelling their growth often become the new incumbents for their industry as they are able to embrace the regulatory overhead (and sometimes provide expert guidance in its creation) that erects new barriers for entrants or smaller companies to overcome.

Just look at the highly regulated traditional financial world. We saw fintech initially emerge as a market segment planning to disrupt the financial status quo. However, it has evolved into a segment where many of these new businesses have struggled to find profitable business models other than the selling of loan products. In addition, fintech companies still end up using much of the financial industry's traditional payment and settlement infrastructure they had hoped to replace. It's a highly regulated and complex ecosystem for good reason.

This is why this period of rapid experimentation and growth is such an important period in which to embrace the opportunity to learn how you can capitalise on blockchain and DLT technology. Otherwise, before you know it, the landscape will have evolved to become another established industry with its winners and losers, with those at the top of the pile capturing a significant slice of the pie. You just need to make sure you get there before it's too late.

Free PR for your work

The saying 'no news is good news' is not a good strategy to keep your investors happy, and naturally news of your company engaging in activities with blockchain is likely to be seen as a positive initiative by these groups.

Even if there are concerns about the potential for sunk cost due to evaluating the wrong opportunity or it not providing the payoff you had hoped for, where your organisation does not move beyond the discovery phase, you will still have learned great lessons in this work. This, of course, will create positive press about how your organisation has embraced blockchain.

No doubt if you aren't using it, investors or other members of your leadership teams will be asking about it simply because of the significant growth of the industry. Being able to bring some news to market about your organisation will help satisfy those pushing for it, while also generating a wider buzz about the work your company is doing, which will in turn attract positive sentiment.

This can also extend to staff and potential hires who will no doubt prefer to be aligned with forward-thinking companies that are embracing the opportunities presented by this technology, as opposed to simply viewing it as a threat.

How agile is your vessel?

I like to think about business in terms of ocean analogies, whether in terms of picking the best wave of innovation to paddle into, catch and ride, taking businesses to new heights. Or a ship navigating its way through treacherous seas to take you from one port to another.

Taking the ship analogy further, smaller firms are like yachts – able to move quickly and change tack in response to the conditions presented to them. The larger organisations are more akin to containerships carrying significant value on board and once they're on a path, its orders of magnitude make it harder for them to change direction in response to the environmental conditions around them.

This container ship mindset can also be accompanied by the perception that change in their industry is slow. However, the business environment, like the ocean, is constantly changing; every once in a while, extraordinary events or outliers come along that force organisations to respond rapidly. In extreme cases they otherwise have to turn too quickly and risk capsizing.

CASE STUDY: BANKING ON BLOCKCHAIN

The banking giant J.P. Morgan recognised early the opportunity that blockchain presented to its business and in November 2016 released its own version of Ethereum. Named Quorum, it provided additional privacy, performance and permissioning capabilities on top of Ethereum to meet the needs of private blockchain networks.

Although the platform was broadly compatible with Ethereum technology, it still lacked specific feature support.

Having already released the popular blockchain library Web3j by this point, the Web3 Labs team adapted it to support the privacy features of Quorum to make the platform available to an even wider group of users in enterprises around the world.[79]

Working alongside the Quorum team, Web3 Labs assisted J.P. Morgan in building out its ecosystem to make the platform more accessible to users.

Although this was relatively early in the adoption of blockchain technology, having one of the largest banks in the world embracing the opportunity provided by the technology shows just how agile these organisations can be when they need to be.

Network effects

Regardless of the perceived rate of change in your industry or organisation, that's not a good reason to hold off making some calculated bets on the opportunity. The blockchain industry is growing at a staggering rate: the internet took seven and a half years to go from 130 million to a billion users,[80] and the Bitcoin network alone is projected to reach that number by 2025. This doesn't include all of the other popular blockchain networks and the decentralised applications being built on top of them.

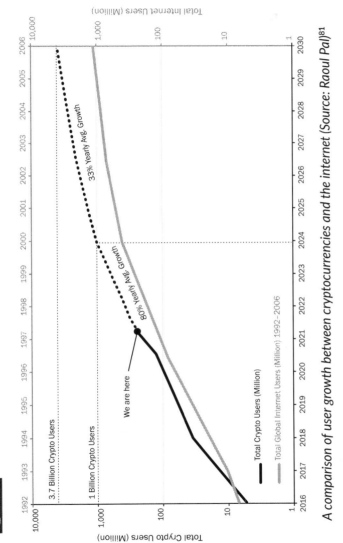

A comparison of user growth between cryptocurrencies and the internet (Source: Raoul Pal)[81]

If you need more convincing, just look at the rate at which the underlying cryptocurrencies have gained value due to the network effect of their adoption.[82] A $2,000 investment into the public Ethereum crowd sale back in 2014 is worth $1.2 million.[83] This staggering rate of growth reflects the perceived value increase of the Ethereum network. This can be characterised by Metcalfe's law, which states that the value of a network is proportional to the square of the number of connected users to the network.[84] Or more explicitly, the value of a blockchain network increases alongside the number of active users on the network, where an active user could be a node on the network, an active wallet or a decentralised application. Strictly speaking, although the value of a cryptocurrency whose purpose is to provide utility to a blockchain network shouldn't be a direct reflection of the value of the network, the applications built on top of it should be. But for the time being speculation on the price of cryptocurrencies seems to be tied to the popularity of the underlying networks, for instance ether in the case of Ethereum.

It is this notion of value attached to blockchain networks via their tokens, and the drivers of that value, that is a core tenet of token economics. Blockchain networks should create desirable outcomes for all network participants via incentive mechanisms. This includes those participants holding tokens for interacting with the network, and those responsible for validating transactions and maintaining the security and integrity of the actual network. Getting this balance right is hard, which is why there is so much interest in token economic models.

With these rates of growth, the speed with which block-chain can change industries is going to be staggering. Taking some well-placed bets on the technology isn't a gamble, it's an insurance policy to help protect your organisation from wider disruption.

This technology has already created a completely new type of investable asset class in the form of cryptocurrencies that are offering investors better returns then almost every other asset class (there is a lot of price volatility, but that comes with any type of frontier asset).

The DeFi ecosystem has spun up almost overnight offering yields on assets that simply are not possible in conventional banking and financial markets. Holders of leading stablecoin USDC, a dollar-pegged digital currency whose investors include Goldman Sachs and Fidelity, can earn yields of over 8% from leading DeFi lending platforms.[85]

Likewise, the NFT ecosystem, which has seen digital art exchanging hands for eye-watering amounts, artist Beeple's *Everydays* being the most famous at $67.3 million,[86] which one could argue in many instances cannot be justified. The underlying technology is sound and provides a digitally provable record of ownership and provenance that simply was not available previously without using a centralised provider.

These are the widely cited examples of what's happening in the public domain. In the world of enterprise blockchain there is just as much activity, which we'll talk more about shortly.

Of course, with all of the public assets I've outlined there is risk, but I'm not here to advise you on whether you should be getting exposure to cryptocurrencies, stablecoins and embracing DeFi and NFTs. The point is that these new infrastructures and ecosystems are being created at an unprecedented rate, creating new types of value for those participating in these ecosystems, and they are disrupting industries already.

Summary

Blockchain provides a common layer that enables organisations to take the internal state associated with business transactions and externalise it, simplifying interorganisational communication and trust.

Although regulation exists for many types of digital asset such as cryptocurrencies, it is still being established for the fast-moving landscape of DeFi. This enables DeFi and other recent innovations to evolve quickly, but they may be impacted as regulation emerges to help protect consumers.

Network effects, such as those characterised by Metcalfe's law, helped the internet, World Wide Web and social networks grow very quickly. We're seeing similar rates of adoption with blockchain technology.

14

Finding The Right Resources

In the same way that we are always trying to find the optimum combination of health, time and wealth in life, usually with far too little time, you will likely feel held back to some degree due to a lack of funding, staff or expertise to achieve what you'd like to be able to do with blockchain or DLT in your organisation.

Being able to secure the right level of funding will come down to having the right stakeholders on board to sponsor any new initiative. Exactly how you can prepare for such a conversation we cover in more detail in the final chapter. But unless you're in the fortunate position of already having funds earmarked for innovation at your disposal it's something you'll probably need to go after, which we'll be discussing further in this chapter.

The rise of the blockchain expert

At the end of 2019, LinkedIn published a report[87] on the most in-demand skills that companies are looking for. Not only did blockchain make the list for the first time that year, it also topped it, ahead of cloud computing, AI, UX design, business analysis and sales.

And then, in the aftermath of the Covid-19 pandemic, as we discussed earlier in Chapter 5, blockchain has enjoyed a meteoric rise and taken it to places never thought possible. This has had the effect of squeezing what was already considered the world's most in-demand hard skillset; now all companies, whether leading blockchain companies or high-growth startups, are struggling in the war for talent.

What this means on a practical level is that it's not necessarily obvious how to find the right resources you need to deliver on blockchain initiatives.

Upskill risks

If you have some staff resources at your disposal you could look to upskill them on the technology and work with training providers. However, the reality is that blockchain brings together concepts from distributed systems and cryptography and, unless you have staff who have expertise in these areas, you're looking at a minimum six-month time horizon to turn your staff into knowledgeable resources who will have the right mindset and understanding required to build a blockchain or DLT application correctly.

There is also the real risk that once they've achieved a good grounding in what's possible with the technology, they will chase a more lucrative opportunity, or decide to create their own DeFi protocol or NFT-based products. Recruiters on platforms like LinkedIn constantly approach anyone with blockchain in their skillset and, trust me, there's only so many times you can put up with a conversation that starts with, 'I wasn't looking for another job, but this person just reached out to me on LinkedIn and it was really interesting what they were doing.' This means that if you do invest more internally in the technology, in the current climate those staff become a flight risk.

This skills shortage will become less acute over time, as technical talent will start gravitating towards upskilling themselves in blockchain and DLT technology to help fill the abundance of opportunities that are available. So while it may be tricky at the moment to find the right people, it won't stay that way for ever.

Build partnerships

One potential such solution to these expertise and staffing dilemmas lies in finding the right partners to work with, partners that are recognised for their contributions and expertise in the domain.

It's important that in finding these partners, you choose neutral entities who share your values. This enables you to build trust, have transparent conversations on which solutions best serve the needs of your business and appreciate their motivations, too. There is a lot of tribalism within the public blockchains and cryptocurrency communities: at one extreme, bitcoin maximalists describe any cryptocurrency that isn't bitcoin as a 'shitcoin'; and at the other end, are those who believe that networks like Bitcoin and Ethereum are fundamentally flawed and doomed to failure, but have built a superior technology that is the solution.

This tribalism does extend to some degree to enterprise deployments. After all, if someone has invested heavily in a specific blockchain project, why wouldn't they want to see the community around it grow, reinforcing the network effect of their favourite platform, as we spoke about in the last chapter.

This means that while any delivery partner you engage with may have specific platforms they mostly work with, they shouldn't exclude other leading platforms from the discussion, unless they can provide a convincing argument that makes sense to you in the process. The landscape of new platforms and technologies is constantly shifting and it's important that the right balance is achieved with what you embrace.

Referring back to our principles of successful blockchain deployments, content at web3labs.com/resources will be helpful before you engage in any such discussions with a potential partner.

CASE STUDY: PRIVACY IN ENTERPRISE ETHEREUM

The Ethereum client Hyperledger Besu is a key component of ConsenSys' Quorum blockchain offering. Quorum is the leading Enterprise Ethereum variant, which was originally created by J.P. Morgan.

ConsenSys wanted to be able to strengthen its privacy offering in Besu, to meet the privacy requirements of the organisations this technology was built to cater for. I had been involved in the early days of Quorum in 2017, making contributions to its secure enclave technology.[88] We discussed in Chapter 13 how we had adapted Web3j for the platform and it made sense to bring Web3 Labs in to work as a partner with ConsenSys.

The Web3 Labs team were responsible for delivering a number of the privacy enhancements in Besu, such as privacy groups and the ability to dynamically modify participants in private transactions. This enabled Besu to meet the privacy needs of ConsenSys' enterprise customers. We were also able to incorporate these features into our Web3j library, ensuring that it was straightforward for developers to integrate these enhancements into their enterprise applications.

As a project that is governed under the Hyperledger project, it is in the interests of all to ensure there are multiple organisations that can support and maintain these blockchain technologies, and with Web3 Labs supporting Hyperledger Besu it helped broaden the ecosystem around the project.

What about our existing partners?

What about offshore software companies that are experts in AI, blockchain and IoT? I'm sure, like me, you're constantly inundated with connection requests from companies with blockchain experts who can deliver your application at a fraction of the cost of what other organisations may quote. Or perhaps some of the providers that your company works with who have already gone through the vendor procurement process claim to have resources that can help.

This may be the case, but, as I've argued earlier, one of the big challenges with building out decentralised applications is that all too often people approach blockchain and DLT as just another storage technology; at one level they may be able to build a so-called decentralised application, but the reality is that they're stuck in their traditional technology paradigms because they lack the nuanced understanding of how one should approach decentralised technology.

Getting this wrong is an expensive mistake to make. While such individuals may be technically competent, the only way to be sure they're approaching the delivery of the application in the right manner is to have people with a strong track record of blockchain and DLT technology involved at the outset.

Acquisitions

Of course, one option, if you have good cash reserves, is to simply wait for an attractive business to emerge and swoop in, buy up their staff and intellectual property, allowing you to rapidly exploit blockchain within your business.

This may bring with it the headline your investors want to see, but whether such an acquisition works out in the long run is less certain; the failure rate of merger and acquisition deals lies between 70% and 90%.[89] Staff attrition rates are often high too, and integrating this new business with your existing is time-consuming and complex. If your organisation and this new one have complementary cultures, that will certainly help, but it's often not as sure a bet as many would like.

Ecosystem funds

These struggles of obtaining talent are restricted not only to companies trying to create decentralised applications, but also the technology companies providing the block-chain platforms for organisations to build on top of.

In the first quarter of 2021 alone, approximately $2.6 billion was obtained in funding by 129 blockchain and crypto startups – $300 million more than was received in the whole of 2020.[90] This has produced a huge number of cash-rich startups competing for talent and further increasing the competition.

The technology companies creating new protocols or communities recognise this and, as a result, many are creating funds running into tens of millions of dollars to help build their ecosystems. As a result of these initiatives, lots of high-quality, open-source software is being built to make these platforms more accessible to users.

While working with these blockchain protocol companies is a slightly different proposition to exploiting new business opportunities with the technology, it illustrates how the shortage of blockchain skills can impact all organisations working with blockchain. It also ensures that businesses aren't simply building on top of foundations laid by others, but are contributing directly to those foundations and helping to grow the whole ecosystem.

CASE STUDY: ECOSYSTEM DEVELOPMENT WITH WEB3J

The Corda platform by R3 is a permissioned DLT platform built for enterprises enabling them to transact directly with one another with strict privacy in place.

One area that users of its product struggled with was the ease with which new decentralised applications can be built and tested on the platform.

R3 was aware of the number of people who were working with our open-source library Web3j for integrating with Ethereum, and were interested in finding a mechanism by which Web3j could work with Corda. They partnered with Web3 Labs to create a version of the Web3j library that could plug into Corda.

Our engineers built out a new version of Web3j that reduced not only the barriers to entry to working with

Corda, but also provided new end-to-end testing facilities for developers that had not previously been available, enabling them to easily simulate deployments that mirrored their live environments locally.[91]

This work was a win-win for R3; not only did it enable the company to get infrastructure built by a partner to support its platform, which broadens the reach of their platform ecosystem, it also enabled its engineering teams to remain focused on its core product development and expertise, strengthening the Corda offer.

What is the optimum?

So, where does this leave you in finding the resources you require? Unfortunately, apart from financial woes it is likely to be a struggle to build the right expertise overnight.

Fortunately, there are focused companies founded on the belief that a lack of expertise or understanding shouldn't be a barrier in embracing blockchain technology. And that in order for it to fulfil its potential and enable organisations to appreciate first-hand what it can do for them, there needs to be the right enterprise-focused product ecosystems such as integration libraries and business analytics tools that can help normalise the technology within these organisations. This is supported by partnerships with multiple platform providers, which ensures that the appropriate tool is always selected for the problem in hand.

The last thing your company needs is to feel that a service provider doesn't understand your business or has just added blockchain and DLT to the long list of emerging technologies you can work with. You need to find niche providers that, at the very least, can ensure you are on the right track, or provide an end-to-end service taking you from discovery through to deployment.

Summary

Blockchain is a highly sought-after skillset. If you don't have appropriate resources in your organisation, you can look to work partners who do have the expertise.

The following checklist will help you to vet potential partners. You should expect to see that they meet most, if not all, criteria:

- Membership or contributions to relevant blockchain industry organisations such as Hyperledger, the Enterprise Ethereum Alliance, Decentralised Identity Foundation, EU Blockchain Observatory and Forum and others mentioned in the Resources section at the end of the book

- Free blockchain products you can trial, or open-source products that are free to use

- Regular publication of genuinely useful content and thought leadership via social media platforms, blog posts, podcasts or video content

- Partnerships with leading blockchain companies such as R3, ConsenSys and IBM, or well-known public protocols mentioned in the Resources section

- Staff speaking at relevant industry conferences or events

- Relevant case studies supporting their work

- Experience leading digital transformation initiatives

15

How To Pitch Blockchain To Your Board

It's crunch time. You're sold on the potential opportunity of blockchain and you see great things for your organisation if you can get the right support from decision-makers. The only issue now is that you need to get those people on board.

It's impossible not to be captivated by what is taking place in the cryptocurrency and blockchain ecosystem, once you move beyond the financial speculation narrative and focus on the game-changing value being created there.

Whether it's your board of directors, management committee, leadership team or investors, you need to ensure that not only do you get them behind your vision, but that you excite them about the new opportunities blockchain or DLT can provide for your business.

In this chapter I will lay out how you can successfully pitch the opportunity to those key decision-makers and provide suitable context to help get them over the line. This process consists of eight steps.

The eight steps to a successful pitch

Step 1: Preparation

Before you present to an audience of key decision-makers, it's important to do your homework. You should have identified the decision-makers, and the potential advocates or champions among them. Ideally you will have had an opportunity to meet with and brief them on what you're trying to achieve. You may wish to incorporate parts of the subsequent steps in this process before you do it for real, so as to have their validation in advance of any formal presentation.

They are likely to voice concerns or highlight any risks associated with what you're proposing; you should take these on board and ensure you address or mitigate these concerns in your actual presentation.

Depending on the willingness of these stakeholders to embrace blockchain technology, you may also need to invest time educating them on blockchain so they really appreciate the opportunity. You will likely need to over-communicate the message to them. Bringing in external speakers who are working with the technology can help add credibility to it here. You may even want to put on an internal blockchain event to build this momentum.

Performing these preparatory steps is crucial; by the time you actually present to them you should have an idea of the questions they are likely to ask and have your response ready.

Step 2: Use the right format

A slide deck tends to be the default format, as it's a visual asset that can be fairly easily digested. However, do consider creative approaches that could be used to explain what you're trying to achieve.

Blockchain is a complex topic for many; you may feel the need to provide a primer to simplify it. In the first part of the book, I explained a blockchain in terms of an accounting ledger, and decentralised file storage in terms of a will and testament – real-world concepts that should help most people understand a complex topic. You could incorporate other sources such as online videos. One great example is the BBC's video 'How do crypto-currencies work?'.[92]

Whatever your approach, the most important message to communicate is what can be achieved. So if there's a mechanism of demonstrating the business outcome, this should trump any formats that pull the audience into the weeds of what's happening behind the scenes. One person I know used a game of sudoku to demonstrate to their board how a blockchain privacy technology could be used to serve the needs of their organisation.

For background, you could provide supplementary material such as this book or links to some of the resources I've included. After all, one of the primary goals of this book is to help people envision what's possible here (I may even be able to arrange some free copies for you). Keep in mind that the audience is likely to be time-poor and unlikely to read such resources unless they arouse their curiosity.

If possible, use a designer to help ensure that your deck isn't like every other deck the audience sees. There may be constraints with any corporate branding you need to make use of, but that doesn't mean it isn't worth the time finding someone who can help make it shine. A worksheet is available on our website, www.web3labs.com/innovators.

Step 3: Build the vision

You want to bring your audience on board with your vision. This isn't a solo effort; you want them to feel compelled to come on this journey with you, so they are as much a part of it as you are.

Whether your vision is addressing costly problems in the business (such as platform outages, authenticity guarantees of data being presented in reports from subsidiaries, reducing data reconciliations, intermediary dependencies), or opportunities (such as asset tokenisation or new product or service launches) that address problems outside of your organisation, it's important that you clearly articulate the problem and proposed solution in terms they will understand of the benefits to your audience and organisation in terms they will understand.

For this reason it's crucial to know your audience. Understand what areas of the business they are interested in and be clear on what the likely upside is for them. This will help get them on board.

If you don't have a specific problem or solution you want to focus on, it's probably best to hold off proceeding until you at least have some potential direction to take.

Step 4: Why now is the right time

At this stage you want to excite your audience about the impact blockchain and DLT technology is having, and sow the seed that now is the perfect time to do this. It takes time to build momentum and capabilities, so you need them to act now. It helps here to have some well-researched, trusted sources of information you can use.

Some of the standout sources include:

- Market intelligence firm IDC forecast in 2021 that global spending on blockchain solutions would reach nearly $19 billion in 2024,[93] with growth in 2021 showing an increase of 50% over 2020. They expect this growth to continue at a compound annual growth rate (CAGR) of 48% over the next five years.

- Since 2019, *Forbes* magazine has been publishing its annual *Blockchain 50*[94] report, which features companies that are leaders in how they are adopting blockchain and DLT technology. To qualify for inclusion in the report, organisations have to have a valuation or annual revenue of at least $1 billion – the companies that matter. The report spans all major industries, so chances are you will be able to find an excellent example of how the leaders in your industry are using this disruptive technology.

In Chapter 8 we discussed the importance of using an evidence-based approach to identify and justify the goals you wish to achieve. While these sources are unfiltered, or non-peer reviewed, they are useful at this stage as you're looking for information that helps sell the broader vision.

The content we produce at Web3 Labs, such as our weekly *This Week in Blockchain* podcast and videos,[95] cover enterprise adoption in addition to the crypto, blockchain protocol, DeFi and NFT industries, so it is a useful source of up-to-date news. Our blockchain opportunities series is also available at web3labs.com/blockchain-opportunities, which also provides some context on the broader applications.

Step 5: The ask

Now that your audience is excited about what you're proposing, it's time to tell them exactly what you need to make this happen. Provided you prepared appropriately, as outlined in step 1, there shouldn't be any big surprises here – it should be more of a formality.

The key figures to articulate are:

- How much it will cost

- How long it will take

- How much money it will save, or revenue it will generate

The final point is no doubt the hardest to address, but if you can find a way to articulate this it will make your pitch much stronger. As you know, determining these figures isn't an exact science – you can only build on top of sensible assumptions.

Step 6: Dispel the common myths

There are various myths that still need to be dispelled when discussing blockchain technology. It amazes me how many people still think that blockchain means the Bitcoin network that uses huge volumes of electricity to operate.

This is why in Part One I dispel common blockchain myths. We've also compiled a number of them on our website at web3labs.com/blockchain-myths.

You'll also want to ensure you have the right resources on board to deliver on the work. We discussed these considerations in the previous chapter, and you should have a strategy in place. The lowest risk strategy is to have a company that can provide end-to-end delivery at a fixed cost.

You can also expand on some of the information you provided in step 4 (why now is the right time) and refer to a couple of case studies that back this up. For this you may select other organisations or competitors in your own industry and discuss the opportunities they've been able to exploit with it. Alternatively, you may be able to find blockchain startups that are building offers that challenge aspects of your core business, which can be helpful in articulating how much this technology is starting to disrupt your industry.

Step 7: How you will make it happen

It's important to wrap up with what the next steps are. Perhaps it's to undertake a blockchain discovery session, or maybe you have an idea of a potential PoC you'd like to undertake. Make sure the next steps are clear. You want to ensure the audience is left feeling:

- Clear about the benefits and costs

- That now is the right time

- Confident that you know how to make this happen

- And, most importantly, excited about the opportunity

There will no doubt need to be further discussions to get everything over the line, but a solid pitch will capture their attention and get them on board.

Step 8: Keep the momentum going

After the presentation, it's important to keep the momentum going. Share the deck with all participants and start drip-feeding helpful content to keep them up to date with the industry and everything that's happening. Referencing some of the resources provided in this book will help. You need to keep this initiative front of mind with stakeholders until you have a clear direction on next steps.

There is no sure-fire formula for success, but if you follow the steps I have outlined here you can be confident that you went about it in the best way to maximise your chances of success.

You should now feel ready to undertake your own blockchain innovation journey!

Summary

Regardless of who the key decision-makers are, you need a strategy to get them behind your vision, and excite them about the new opportunities blockchain or DLT can provide for your business.

The following steps will help you to deliver a compelling pitch:

1. **Preparation:** Identify and meet with key decision-makers in advance.

2. **Use the right format for your audience:** Although a well-presented slide deck looks nice, are there more creative approaches that can explain what you're trying to achieve?

3. **Build the vision:** Get your audience on board with the vision.

4. **Why now is the right time:** Demonstrate all the activity already taking place in industry.

5. **The ask, or what resources you require:** How much it will cost, how long it will take and the impact to your business.

6. **Dispel the common myths:** Address any misconceptions about blockchain.

7. **How you will make it happen:** Clearly outline the next steps.

8. **Keep the momentum going:** Keep this initiative front of mind with your audience until you've got a clear response from them on your ask.

Conclusion

Congratulations on staying with me this far. Hopefully you're feeling inspired by everything we've covered and can appreciate why I was excited to share my thoughts with you.

Having undertaken the journey laid out in Part One, you now know your DApp from DeFi and appreciate not only how Bitcoin and Ethereum created the foundations for much of the current blockchain and DLT landscape, but also where it's taking us, and all of the fantastic places it will take us in the future. Next time blockchain comes up in a discussion, and someone asks your opinion on the matter, you should feel confident that you can provide some context on how the attention it's been getting is justified, and that you can see real ways in which it can benefit your industry.

This macro view of blockchain's place in the world should also be supported by what was covered in Part Two, where I discussed exactly how you can embrace blockchain in your organisation, starting by putting yourself in a parallel universe and turning your organisation inside out to appreciate where it can take you. The real work starts here by undertaking the discovery phase, followed by the subsequent design and deployment phases to take you from having a concept to a live platform supporting your customers.

Prioritising blockchain opportunities on top of everything else you're trying to achieve does present challenges, but Part Three should have helped you appreciate why now is the time to take action and that while some barriers will get in your way, none of them are insurmountable, especially given the potential payoff you could see from placing some conservative bets here.

I've tried to ensure the content in this book is as relevant now as it will be many years down the line. Other than those technologies discussed in case studies, and the foundational networks Bitcoin and Ethereum, I've avoided discussing any of the enterprise platforms or newer blockchain protocols here, as this landscape is constantly changing.

At Web3 Labs we work with a number of different platforms and protocols, and the list of these is evolving with the industry. If you choose to engage us to work with you on your blockchain journey, you will have access to our thinking and expertise to ensure you hit the ground running without having to first evaluate tens or even hundreds of different potential platforms.

It's fair to say that at the time of writing, the significant applications of blockchain technology, such as cryptocurrencies, tokens, DeFi, NFTs and enterprise blockchain, have gained considerable traction. I spend a lot of time thinking about what the next big thing will be, and I can say with confidence that all the great work being done in the field of decentralised identity is likely to have wide-reaching impact in the coming months and years, as it eliminates the reliance on third-party services provided by companies where the user is the product.

Beyond this, I touched briefly on DAOs more in a historical context in Part One, but I believe that with the right safety measures in place the potential for their significant adoption is realistic. The ability to create a decentralised application with its own rules and governance that can serve a specific business or purpose is incredible. Charles Stross' book *Accelerando*[96] paints a vivid, albeit somewhat dystopian, picture of where this notion of businesses as code can take us.

I have only scratched the surface of what is possible with blockchain and DLT and how you can go about innovating with this technology. While the discovery, design and deploy phases discussed here provide a framework for supporting this, there is a lot of material that I cannot cover in a book of this length; after all, I'd rather have written a book you finish than an impressive tome that ends up sitting on a shelf gathering dust.

Next steps

I encourage you now to take concrete action to ensure that you don't let your new-found wisdom and knowledge fall by the wayside.

Take our scorecard

If you're ready to keep the momentum going and embrace blockchain within your organisation, we have a scorecard you can download to assess potential opportunities for your business. This is available at www.web3labs.com/innovators.

Review this book

If you like the book, I'd be really grateful if you can leave a review on Amazon, Goodreads or as a blog post. If you do, please email innovators@web3labs.com with details of the review, and we'll send you an exclusive Blockchain Innovators NFT that we've created.

Subscribe to our podcasts and YouTube channel

To keep up to date with everything that's happening in the space, please subscribe to our *This Week in Blockchain* podcast.

For some interesting dialogue with leaders in the blockchain landscape (many with an enterprise focus), you can subscribe to our *Blockchain Innovators* podcast.[97]

The podcasts are available on all major podcasting platforms.

You can also subscribe to the Web3 Labs YouTube channel, www.youtube.com/c/web3labs, where we host videos of them alongside other useful content, including talks from our events.

Access free resources

We provide a number of free resources on blockchain on the Web3 Labs website at web3labs.com/resources

Connect with me

I also regularly post content and opinion on Twitter, via @ ConorSvensson, and LinkedIn. You can engage with me on both these platforms.

A final word

Remember, you will need to keep an open mind to reap the full rewards of this disruptive technology. I encourage you to keep the following words at the front of mind, from the great philosopher Bruce Lee: *The inability to adapt brings destruction.*[98]

Resources

There's a huge amount of content available on crypto-currency and blockchain; these are some of the sources I recommend for learning more about it and keeping up with the latest developments.

Podcasts

- Web3 Labs owns the *This Week in Blockchain* and *Blockchain Innovators* podcasts: www. weekinblockchain.com and https://podcast.web3labs. com

- Lex Fridman has interviewed a number of leading individuals from the crypto and blockchain space: https://lexfridman.com/podcast

- The a16z podcast provides some great perspectives on crypto and blockchain technology: https://future.a16z.com/a16z-podcast

Videos

- Andreas M. Antonopoulos has a lot of excellent accessible talks on bitcoin and blockchain. I highly recommend his talk on innovation, 'Bitcoin and the Coming Infrastructure Inversion': www.youtube.com/watch?v=KXIaILHl7Rg

- Real Vision Crypto is an excellent free service that provides interviews with many of the most influential people in the crypto and blockchain ecosystems: www.realvision.com/crypto

- Our Web3 Labs YouTube Channel provides a variety of content, including videos of our podcasts and talks from industry leaders from our events: www.youtube.com/c/web3labs

News and opinion

Leading sources:

- CoinDesk is the most popular dedicated crypto and blockchain news site: www.coindesk.com

- *Forbes'* Crypto & Blockchain is a great source for news and opinion. In addition, it publishes a number of industry reports, including *Blockchain 50* each year: www.forbes.com/crypto-blockchain

- The World Economic Forum regularly publishes a lot of useful content as well as thought leadership on blockchain: www.weforum.org/agenda/archive/blockchain

Additional sources:

- The Defiant: https://thedefiant.io

- Decrypt: https://decrypt.co

- The Block: www.theblockcrypto.com

- Cointelegraph: https://cointelegraph.com

Data sources

- Etherscan is the leading blockchain explorer for Ethereum and provides a lot of useful charts about the network and cryptocurrency: https://etherscan.io

- CoinMarketCap is the leading information resource on cryptocurrency and blockchain project market capitalisation. As a rule of thumb, the larger the market capitalisation, the more confidence there is in the underlying project protocol: https://coinmarketcap.com

- CoinGecko is another great resource on market metrics, which also includes statistics on DeFi applications and protocols: www.coingecko.com

- NonFungible provides statistics on the non-fungible token market: https://nonfungible.com

- Amberdata provides high-quality institutional grade crypto and DeFi market data services: https://amberdata.io

Industry organisations

- The Enterprise Ethereum Alliance is creating enterprise-focused standards for Ethereum: https://entethalliance.org

- Hyperledger is an open-source community for enterprise blockchain: www.hyperledger.org

- The InterWork Alliance initiative of the Global Blockchain Business Council is establishing standards for business underpinned by blockchain and DLT: https://interwork.org and https://gbbcouncil.org

- The Decentralized Identity Foundation is creating standards for decentralised identity: https://identity.foundation

- The EU Blockchain Observatory and Forum is a European Commission initiative to accelerate blockchain innovation and the development of the blockchain ecosystem: www.eublockchainforum.eu

- MOBI is creating blockchain standards for the transportation industry: https://dlt.mobi

- The Climate Ledger Initiative, while not an industry organisation per se, does bring together leading organisations focusing on climate initiatives with blockchain: www.climateledger.org

- The *Journal of the British Blockchain Association* is a leading academic journal focused on blockchain: https://jbba.scholasticahq.com

Books

Written by the author of the book that inspired the film *The Social Network [The Accidental Billionaire]*, the following book is an entertaining read about the earlier days of the bitcoin movement and some of those who embraced it including the Winklevoss twins.

- *Bitcoin Billionaires: A true story of genius, betrayal, and redemption*, Ben Mezrich (Little, Brown, 2019)

The author of this book, an academic and subscriber to the Austrian school of economic thought, makes the case for Bitcoin providing a suitable foundation for sound money to be based upon. Whilst I don't agree with some of the arguments presented, he does make a compelling case for why cryptocurrencies exhibit a number of properties to make them a superior store of value than today's fiat currencies. Hence, I do recommend it as essential reading for context on cryptocurrencies as a store of value and a primer on token economics.

- *The Bitcoin Standard: The decentralized alternative to central banking,* Saifedean Ammous (Wiley, 2018)

These two books are great sources on the history of Ethereum and the various characters involved in its development, many of whom have gone on to create the third-generation protocols listed below.

- *Out of the Ether: The amazing story of Ethereum and the $55 million heist that almost destroyed it all,* Matthew MacAdam Leising (Wiley, 2021)

- *The Infinite Machine: How an army of crypto-hackers is building the next internet with Ethereum,* Camila Russo (HarperBus, 2020)

For a run-down of a number of the significant scams that have taken place in crypto, the following book is a great read.

- *Crypto Wars: Faked deaths, missing billions and industry disruption,* Erica Stanford (Kogan Page, 2021)

The following books provide a more technical overview of the leading blockchain platforms.

- *Mastering Bitcoin,* Andreas M. Antonopoulos (O'Reilly, 2nd edition, 2017)

- *Mastering Ethereum: Building smart contracts and DApps,* Andreas M. Antonopoulos and Gavin Wood (Wiley, 2018)

- *Mastering Blockchain,* 3rd edition, Imran Bashir (Packt Publishing, 2020)

Blockchain platforms and technologies

The astounding rate of change in the space ensures that the landscape is likely to look quite different in a few years' time from where it is now. That said, I believe it is worth keeping abreast of a number of projects and technologies.

Protocols

Both the Bitcoin and Ethereum project homepages provide a plethora of resources to learn more; these are available at the following locations:

- Bitcoin: https://bitcoin.org
- Ethereum: https://ethereum.org

While not as popular as Bitcoin and Ethereum, there are a number of other blockchain protocols, typically referred to as third-generation blockchain platforms, with significant traction and communities supporting them. At the time of writing, some of the leading ones include:

- Cardano: https://cardano.org
- Polkadot: https://polkadot.network
- Binance Smart Chain: www.binance.org/en/smartChain

- Solana: https://solana.com

- Avalanche: www.avax.network

- Hedera (although it uses a type of DLT – a directed acyclic graph rather than blockchain): https://hedera.com

There are also protocols focused on scaling the capabilities of the Bitcoin and Ethereum network; at the time of writing, the leading protocols are:

- Lightning Network: https://lightning.network

- Optimism: https://optimism.io

- Polygon: https://polygon.technology

The following projects are of note for the problems they are trying to solve:

- Filecoin is building a decentralised storage network on top of IPFS: https://filecoin.io

- Monero and Zcash are privacy-preserving cryptocurrencies: www.getmonero.org and https://z.cash

While widespread blockchain interoperability is still a moving target, a number of the leading projects focused on this space include:

- Cosmos: https://cosmos.network
- ICON: https://iconrepublic.org
- Wanchain: www.wanchain.org

Polkadot (listed above) also comes in this category.

Enterprise blockchain platforms

For private, permissioned consortia networks, the leading platforms are:

- ConsenSys Quorum (originally created by J.P. Morgan): https://consensys.net/quorum
- Hyperledger Fabric from IBM: www.hyperledger.org/use/fabric
- R3's Corda: www.r3.com/corda-platform

The Baseline Protocol is also notable as a platform using the public Ethereum network to store proofs of events and systems of record associated with business workflows: www.baseline-protocol.org

Decentralised platforms and applications

- Uniswap is the most widely used DEX on Ethereum: https://uniswap.org
- Aave is the leading decentralised lending platform: https://aave.com

- Circle's USDC and Tether's USDT are the leading US dollar-pegged stablecoins: www.circle.com/en/usdc and https://tether.to

- OpenSea is the largest NFT marketplace: https://opensea.io

Glossary

As with any new industry or technology, an abundance of terms and acronyms are being adopted to describe many of the innovations associated with blockchain. This glossary lists many of the common ones you are likely to encounter. Some of these are discussed in this book; others are not, but are included for reference.

Bitcoin The first decentralised digital currency.

Blockchain A decentralised ledger where transactions are grouped together into blocks that are linked together in a cryptographically secure manner and shared with all participants on the network.

BTC The symbol for the bitcoin cryptocurrency.

Consensus algorithm The mechanism by which a network reaches agreement among participant nodes on the network.

DApp A decentralised application running on a blockchain or DLT, typically defined as a smart contract.

Decentralised exchange (DEX) An exchange that allows users to exchange tokens without an intermediary.

Decentralised finance (DeFi) The ecosystem of decentralised applications built on public blockchain networks such as Ethereum, which governs innovations such as stablecoins and decentralised lending, insurance, and exchanges.

Decentralised identifier (DID) A verifiable decentralised identifier that is decoupled from a centralised provider.

Digital twin A digital representation of a real-world asset.

Distributed ledger technology (DLT) A system of record that is distributed across multiple nodes on a network, where transactions are shared among participants on the network.

EIP An Ethereum improvement proposal.

Elliptic curve A type of mathematical curve that underpins public key cryptography.

ERC Ethereum request for comments, an Ethereum standard.

ERC-20 The Ethereum fungible token standard.

ERC-721 The Ethereum non-fungible token standard.

ETH The symbol for the ether cryptocurrency.

Ethereum A blockchain platform for running smart contracts and decentralised applications.

Fungible token A token that is interchangeable with another token.

Gas The fee associated with a blockchain transaction on the Ethereum blockchain.

Hard fork A breaking change to a blockchain protocol.

Initial Coin Offering (ICO) A public token sale for a block-chain protocol or project where the funds are raised by investors investing cryptocurrencies into a smart contract that gives them tokens in return that can be used with the new project or protocol once built.

Initial DEX Offering (IDO) A project token sale that takes place on a decentralised exchange.

Initial Exchange Offering (IEO) A project token sale that takes place on a centralised exchange.

IPFS The Interplanetary Filesystem, a decentralised file storage network.

Launchpad A platform facilitating IDOs with investment pools.

Layer 1 protocols Base blockchain network protocols.

Layer 2 protocols Overlay networks sitting on top of the base protocol that are typically used for scaling or privacy purposes.

Non-fungible token (NFT) A token that is not interchangeable with another token. It represents the unique attributes of something digital or physical that cannot be duplicated.

Off-chain governance A decision-making process that takes place on more conventional channels, not on the blockchain.

On-chain governance A decision-making process for a blockchain protocol that takes place with voting via smart contracts that reside on the associated blockchain.

Peer-to-peer network A decentralised network where resources such as processing and storage are distributed equally among computers (peers) on a network.

Proof of stake (PoS) A consensus algorithm that uses the cryptocurrency holdings of a miner to dictate how frequently they can validate transactions and hence be rewarded by the network. The larger their stake or value of cryptocurrency they are willing to put into the network, the higher the return. Should they act dishonestly, they will be penalised by the network and their stake proportionally reduced as a result.

Proof of work (PoW) A consensus algorithm that requires computational power to solve a computationally hard mathematic problem. This problem is probabilistic in nature, hence the more computation that can be used for it, the higher the likelihood of success. In blockchain networks using PoW consensus, miners are continually competing with one another to solve these problems and select the next group or block of transactions to be added to the blockchain. When a solution is found the miner that found the solution is rewarded in cryptocurrency. Hence the more computational resources and electricity to power the computation a miner has at their disposal, the more likely they are to solve the computational problem and receive a reward. This consensus mechanism comes under heavy criticism for the fact it uses large amounts of electricity to function.

Public key cryptography A type of cryptography that uses public and private keys that enable someone to encrypt or sign a message with a private key, which can only be decrypted or verified using the associated public key.

Security token A token that represents financial value in the project it is associated with.

Security Token Offering (STO) A usually private token sale where security tokens are issued to investors.

Smart contract The application code used to write decentralised applications that run on a blockchain.

Soft fork A backward-compatible change to a blockchain protocol.

Token economics The study of the economic factors and mechanisms that are used to create value in blockchain and cryptocurrency ecosystems.

Utility token A token that is native to a blockchain network or project that provides some utility for users.

Verified credential A credential that has been verified by a third party.

Yield farming The process of lending crypto assets for yield on DeFi platforms.

Zero-knowledge proof A type of cryptographic proof that enables one party to prove to another party that they know the value of a thing without having to share any information apart from the fact they know the value.

Notes

1. www.gold.org/goldhub/data/above-ground-stocks estimates that 201,296 tonnes of gold has been mined throughout history, with a spot price of $1,800 per ounce, giving a market size of $11,594,649,600,000 (or approx. $11.6 trillion).
2. www.reuters.com/technology/nft-sales-volume-surges-25-bln-2021-first-half-2021-07-05
3. https://defipulse.com. Accurate as per September 2021.
4. www.gartner.com/en/doc/3855708-digital-disruption-profile-blockchains-radical-promise-spans-business-and-society
5. Bitcoin with a capital B denotes the Bitcoin protocol, network and community. The cryptocurrency is called bitcoin, with a lowercase b.

6. At the end of 2020, Google's authentication service failed, bringing Google, Gmail and YouTube down for the majority of their users www.theguardian.com/technology/2020/dec/14/google-suffers-worldwide-outage-with-gmail-youtube-and-other-services-down

7. www.cnbc.com/2021/01/08/apples-app-store-had-gross-sales-around-64-billion-in-2020.html

8. It's believed in some circles to have been more than one person.

9. Satoshi Nakamoto, 'Bitcoin: A Peer-to-Peer Electronic Cash System' (2008), www.ussc.gov/sites/default/files/pdf/training/annual-national-training-seminar/2018/Emerging_Tech_Bitcoin_Crypto.pdf

10. See https://ethereum.org/en/whitepaper

11. In computer science circles, general purpose computers are what is known as 'Turing Complete.'

12. www.apple.com/uk/newsroom/2020/06/apples-app-store-ecosystem-facilitated-over-half-a-trillion-dollars-in-commerce-in-2019

13. Ignoring the cryptocurrency mania of 2021.

14. www.uprr.com/aboutup/history/lincoln/nation_trans/index.shtml

15. Refer to the following article for more background: www.infoq.com/news/2017/04/blockchain-cap-theorem

16. Like equities, cryptocurrencies also have abbreviated symbols to describe them; in the case of bitcoin it's BTC and for ether it's ETH. If you want to see what people are saying about them on Twitter, search for them by prefixing a dollar sign such as $BTC and $ETH.

17. The exact ways in which fees are distributed varies from network to network. Ethereum, for example, recently started destroying, or burning, a proportion of fees to ensure that they remained more consistent for users of the network. For further information, read https://github.com/ethereum/EIPs/blob/master/EIPS/eip-1559.md

18. This was at their peak in Q2 2021, after which they dropped significantly. However, at the time of writing Bitcoin's market capitalisation is still over $500 million and Ethereum's over $200 million. https://coinmarketcap.com/coins

19. Strictly speaking this should be referred to as a token.

20. See https://ipfs.io

21. See https://filecoin.io

22. For more information on private blockchain technologies, I encourage you to refer to the following blog post: https://blog.web3labs.com/blockchain-technology-considerations

23. In fact, the ability to create custom coins was one of the driving forces in the creation of Ethereum. Its creator, Vitalik Buterin, was trying to create coloured coins on Bitcoin, but ran into limitations. See Matthew MacAdam Leising, *Out of the Ether: The amazing story of Ethereum and the $55 million heist that almost destroyed it all* (Wiley, 2021)

24. https://eips.ethereum.org/EIPS/eip-20

25. Although the approach taken by the Ethereum community influenced the ICO concept, in Ethereum's case it's referred to as the Ethereum crowd sale.

26. https://twitter.com/bramcohen/status/10759063727
07860480?lang=en

27. For a more detailed primer, see https://
coinmarketcap.com/alexandria/article/a-deep-dive-
into-tokenization

28. www.forbes.com/sites/haileylennon/2021/01/19/
the-false-narrative-of-bitcoins-role-in-illicit-activity

29. See Matthew MacAdam Leising, *Out of the Ether:
The amazing story of Ethereum and the $55 million heist
that almost destroyed it all* (Wiley, 2021) and https://
en.wikipedia.org/wiki/The_DAO_(organization) for
more information

30. We use Ethereum to refer to the Ethereum network –
the terms are interchangeable.

31. See https://eips.ethereum.org/EIPS/eip-721

32. See www.cryptokitties.co

33. https://tether.to/wp-content/uploads/2021/04/tether-
assurance-mar-2021-2.pdf; www.circle.com/en/usdc

34. This will change in due course as this lack of
regulation has the attention of regulators globally.

35. For the curious, I encourage you to refer to this
excellent primer and explanation of a couple of
highly profitable exploits they've used: https://
hackingdistributed.com/2020/03/11/flash-loans

36. 'Top 100 DeFi Coins by Market Capitalization',
Coingecko.com (14 November 2021), available at
www.coingecko.com/en/defi. Reproduced with
permission.

37. The service provided by https://haveibeenpwned.
com is excellent in notifying you of data breaches
and how they affect you.

38. In Europe, for instance, six countries have signed up to the eIDAS Regulation. See https://digital-strategy.ec.europa.eu/en/news/national-eids-six-countries-available-eu-citizens-use-cross-border

39. I would love to see a solution that prevents malicious actors from taking your email address and being able to sign up to any number of email lists. This would save the world billions of hours in lost productivity, but that's a topic for another day.

40. See www.w3.org/TR/did-core

41. Drummond Reed, 'Decentralized Identifiers (DIDs): The Fundamental Building Block of Self-Sovereign Identity (SSI)' (Slideshare, 2018), available at www.slideshare.net/SSIMeetup/decentralized-identifiers-dids-the-fundamental-building-block-of-selfsovereign-identity-ssi. Reproduced under CC BY-SA 4.0, https://creativecommons.org/licenses/by-sa/4.0

42. www.officialdata.org/us/inflation/1800?amount=1

43. https://en.wikipedia.org/wiki/Generation_Z#/media/File:Generation_timeline.svg

44. https://news.stanford.edu/news/2005/june15/jobs-061505.html

45. Matthew Walker, *Why We Sleep* (Penguin Books, 2018)

46. See www.youtube.com/watch?v=YHjYt6Jm5j8 for an entertaining take on Bitcoin

47. Yorke Rhodes at Enterprise Ethereum Alliance Virtual Meetup, July 2021, www.youtube.com/watch?v=lVzNVNfZlDY

48. See www.cio.gov/policies-and-priorities/evidence-based-policymaking

49. Naseem Naqvi and Mureed Hussain, 'Evidence-Based Blockchain: Findings from a Global Study of Blockchain Projects and Start-up Companies', p6, The JBBA, 1 September 2020, available at https://doi.org/10.31585/jbba-3-2-(8)2020. Reproduced with permission.

50. See https://doaj.org

51. See www.ssrn.com

52. Naseem Naqvi and Mureed Hussain, 'Evidence-Based Blockchain: Findings from a Global Study of Blockchain Projects and Start-up Companies', p6–8, *The JBBA*, 1 September 2020, available at https://doi.org/10.31585/jbba-3-2-(8)2020. Reproduced with permission.

53. See https://docs.baseline-protocol.org

54. See https://equipmentconnect.co.uk

55. For more background, see Eric Ries, *The Lean Startup: How today's entrepreneurs use continuous innovation to create radically successful businesses* (New York: Crown Business, 2011)

56. See www.scaledagileframework.com

57. Hubspot provides some excellent resources on go-to-market strategies at https://blog.hubspot.com/sales/gtm-strategy

58. We discuss some of the available options in the Platform Deployment section of the following article: https://blog.web3labs.com/how-to-choose-the-right-blockchain-development-team. ING also published a useful paper on this: https://new.ingwb.com/binaries/content/assets/insights/

themes / distributed-ledger-technology / dlt_nodes_
outsourcing_considerations.pdf
59. https: / / unstats.un.org / wiki / display /
InteropGuide / Introduction; www.climateledger.org /
resources / CLI_Report_2020_state-and-trends.pdf
60. See https: / / iconrepublic.org
61. X.509 is the widely accepted standard for these
public key certificates.
62. We discuss some of the technologies available for
cryptographic key management in the Security
section of the following article: https: / / blog.
web3labs.com / how-to-choose-the-right-blockchain-
development-team
63. For a helpful discussion on proxies on the Ethereum
platform, you can refer to the following blog post:
https: / / blog.openzeppelin.com / proxy-patterns
64. For a great list of high-profile outages and their
causes, see https: / / github.com / danluu / post-
mortems
65. The Bitcoin network has had two outages, one in
2010, the other in 2013. The Ethereum network has
not had an outage since launch.
66. This exact thing happened in November
2020 when the widely used Infura Ethereum
infrastructure provider had a major outage. See
www.theblockcrypto.com / post / 84232 / ethereum-
infrastructure-provider-infura-is-down
67. There are DLTs that are not blockchains, such as
R3's Corda technology, which approach privacy
differently to conventional blockchains such as
Ethereum. However, Ethereum variants such as

ConsenSys' Quorum provide their own additional privacy measures.

68. See https://hbr.org/2016/11/why-diverse-teams-are-smarter

69. The type of problem is referred to as computationally hard – it requires a lot of effort on the part of the graphics card to generate random numbers until it finds one that provides a solution within a set range to a mathematical function. Once a solution has been found, it can easily be verified by other computers.

70. You can view the presentation I gave to the Ethereum Sydney Community on how you can build a mining rig, from back when Ether was hovering at a paltry $15, at www.slideshare.net/ConorSvensson/ether-mining-101-v2

71. Ramesh Ramadoss, 'The Role of the IWA in the Standardization Landscape', InterWork Alliance (no date), https://interwork.org/the-role-of-the-iwa-in-the-standardization-landscape

72. The specifications are available at https://entethalliance.org/technical-specifications

73. For a more detailed discussion, I encourage you to refer to the World Economic Forum's excellent guide on consortium formation: https://widgets.weforum.org/blockchain-toolkit/consortium-formation/index.html

74. See Clayton M. Christensen, *The Innovator's Dilemma: When new technologies cause great firms to fail* (Boston, Mass: Harvard Business School Press, 1997)

75. www.reutersevents.com/supplychain/technology/tesla-market-cap-surpasses-next-five-largest-automotive-companies-combined

76. https://en.wikipedia.org/wiki/General_Motors_EV1

77. If you require more resources on why having an innovation strategy is important, the following article from the *Harvard Business Review* is excellent: https://hbr.org/2015/06/you-need-an-innovation-strategy

78. See Tim Wu, *The Master Switch: The rise and fall of information empires* (New York: A.A. Knopf, 2011)

79. See https://github.com/web3j/web3j-quorum

80. www.nasdaq.com/articles/can-bitcoin-grow-faster-than-the-internet-2021-05-07

81. Raoul Pal (@RaoulGMI), 'This concept in crypto can be best represented...' (24 May 2021), https://twitter.com/RaoulGMI/status/1396837073202532357/photo/1. Reproduced with permission.

82. This video by Raoul Pal unpacks from a macro perspective how the network effect of blockchain adoption has driven their price growth: www.realvision.com/shows/expert-view-crypto/videos/the-exponential-age-cryptos-fast-and-furious-rise

83. This is using a conservative price of $2,000 per Ether; during this latest growth cycle it passed $4,000.

84. Metcalfe's Law was originally created for telecommunications networks, but has since been applied to fax machines, the World Wide Web and social media. For more information refer to https://en.wikipedia.org/wiki/Metcalfe%27s_law

85. https://defirate.com/usdc. The leading platforms Aave and BlockFi were providing these rates at the time of writing.

86. See www.christies.com/features/Monumental-collage-by-Beeple-is-first-purely-digital-artwork-NFT-to-come-to-auction-11510-7.aspx

87. See www.linkedin.com/business/learning/blog/learning-and-development/most-in-demand-skills-2020

88. See https://github.com/ConsenSys/constellation/commits?author=conor10

89. See https://hbr.org/2011/03/the-big-idea-the-new-ma-playbook

90. CB Insights via Bloomberg, reported at https://cointelegraph.com/news/vc-funds-bullish-on-crypto-increase-investment-in-blockchain-startups

91. See https://blog.web3labs.com/how-to-create-an-awesome-developer-experience-for-corda and www.r3.com/videos/creating-an-awesome-developer-experience-on-corda-web3-labs

92. www.bbc.co.uk/news/av/technology-43026143

93. See www.idc.com/getdoc.jsp?containerId=prUS47617821

94. The 2021 edition is available at www.forbes.com/sites/michaeldelcastillo/2021/02/02/blockchain-50/?sh=30608899231c

95. See www.weekinblockchain.com

96. Charles Stross, *Accelerando* (New York: Ace Books, 2005)

97. See https://podcast.web3labs.com

98. Bruce Lee, *Striking Thoughts* (Tuttle Publishing, 2002)

99. See www.skylarks.charity/page/send-advice-service

Acknowledgements

Firstly, and most importantly of all, I'd like thank my wonderful wife Leyla and my children for providing the foundation upon which everything else in my life is achieved. My awesome parents, siblings and the wider O'Dea and Svensson clans whom I've been very fortunate to have in my life.

Everyone at Web3 Labs who has ridden through the ups and downs – the pandemic created new challenges for us as a business, but we came out stronger as a result.

I have to extend a special thanks to Nancy, who keeps so many plates spinning in the air at Web3 Labs while also supporting my work in so many ways. You really are the hidden star behind the scenes.

As a keen consumer of books, being able to give back to the reading community is something I've wanted to do for a long time. I need to thank Daniel Priestley and Dent for giving me the push I needed to make it happen. I'd also like to extend my gratitude to Lucy McCarraher and Joe Gregory for the structure they provided me with for writing the book, which was invaluable when trying to juggle the demands of running a growing business and having a young family to support.

I'd like to thank my draft reviewers, who took a significant chunk of time out of their schedules to provide the detailed feedback and perspective I needed to refine this book; Harry Winstain, Alex Banks, Mariana Gomez de la Villa, Christian Felde and Mohamed Elshami – I really appreciate it.

Raoul Pal for getting on board with writing the foreword to this book and Conor O'Dea for bringing us together. I asked right around the time Real Vision was closing its Series C financing round, so I am especially grateful that you made the time.

Finally, everyone we've had the opportunity to work with over the years. It's these opportunities that have enabled us to build solutions that we're proud to be associated with, and present learnings from here. Thanks also to anyone who has ever used Web3j. It's always incredible to connect with users and fans of the library.

An Afterword on Neurodiversity

Neurodiversity is a term used to positively promote qualities of those viewed as having neurodevelopment differences. It supports the notion that when it comes to the human condition, 'one size does not fit all' and recognises and celebrates everyone's unique abilities and neurodevelopmental differences.

In so doing, neurodiversity rejects cultural negativity that has for too long been associated with neural variations. It does not seek a 'cure' for neurodevelopmental differences but an increased understanding – and reimagining of our understandings – around, for example, autism, dyslexia, dyspraxia and epilepsy, viewing them merely as a natural variation in the human genome. Whilst the term applies to a range of neurodiverse people, my specific focus is on its application to autism/Asperger's Syndrome.

Unfortunately, in many parts of the world there is still inadequate awareness of neurodiversity and most educational establishments lack the resources and understanding of how best to support neurodivergent individuals.

At one end of the spectrum are milder forms of autism such as Asperger's Syndrome, which in some instances is associated with highly successful people who have managed to turn it into a superpower – Elon Musk and Dan Ackroyd being two cases in point. But for every Elon and Dan, there are many more for whom being a normal member of society is simply impossible.

The challenges don't just lie with the education systems, workplace and life at home, but also in building greater awareness in society of where parents or carers of those who are neurodiverse can get support. Unfortunately, in some instances children with more severe neurodiversity challenges are taken out of school and parents are stuck trying to raise them alone, unaware of any support networks that they can tap into.

We know that no two people are alike, but far too many aspects of our society are set up to benefit those who thrive in exams, team sports and social environments while others are marginalised. Although racial, physical and gender inclusion is slowly gaining the wider support and acceptance it deserves, neurological inclusion remains a fringe topic as it requires many people and organisations to fundamentally reassess how they interact and engage with people who are neurodiverse. The challenge to society is that neurodiversity may or may not present subtly. For example, many of our social interactions are built on shared assumptions of understandings that we frequently need to challenge. To give a simple but fundamental example: the interpretation of tone of voice, facial expressions, nuances etc may not register with the person we're speaking with, and the need to reassess our approaches to social engagement is very important to their inclusion – hopefully reducing the need for that person to go through the discomfort of having to 'mask' in these social situations.

From a personal perspective, attention deficit hyperactivity disorder (ADHD), dyslexia, dyspraxia and autism spectrum condition (ASC), are neurodevelopmental differences close to home as they directly affect my family.

It is for this reason that I believe it is important to support initiatives that can positively assist those who are neurodiverse. As such, all author proceeds from sales of this book will go to support and help grow Skylarks' Special Education Needs and Disabilities (SEND) Advice Service.[99] Skylarks is a charity that provides activities and therapies for children with disabilities and additional needs.

Their SEND Advice Service offers free, impartial support and information to parents and young people with special education needs. Frequently, parents of children with additional educational needs face an uphill battle in getting additional classroom support. This service can make that difference between a child being excluded from school, for example for being disruptive, versus a child or young person receiving provision which allows them to flourish. I believe a lot of societal problems stem from people not receiving the support they need in their earlier years, hence my ability to help champion this free service is of great importance to me.

With time and the right support, it is my hope that our societies can adapt to ensure the many different forms of neurodiversity can thrive. After all, many neurodivergent people bring their own superpowers that can benefit us all, be that through the different perspectives, expertise or focus they have, or even through simple things like joy, singlemindedness and the positivity they bring. My firm belief is that embracing neurodiversity will enhance all our lives.

The Author

Conor is the founder and CEO of Web3 Labs, a blockchain technology company. He is also the host of the *Blockchain Innovators* podcast.

Web3 Labs works with large organisations to deliver applications that improve trust and authenticity of data and assets. Its clients include Microsoft, J.P. Morgan and Vodafone. It also works with leading blockchain companies and protocols to develop their ecosystems and platforms. The organisations Web3 Labs has worked with include ConsenSys, R3, the Open Application Network, the Ethereum Foundation and ICON.

Web3 Labs was a finalist in Microsoft's Partner of the Year 2020 Awards.

Conor is the former chair of the standards working group at the Enterprise Ethereum Alliance, responsible for publishing the world's first Enterprise Ethereum standards. He is currently vice-chair of the InterWork Framework Working Group at the Global Blockchain Business Council, has previously served on the Baseline Protocol Technical Steering Committee and was involved in the Hyperledger Climate Accounting Special Interest Group.

He originally stumbled upon blockchain in 2016 when he started learning about Ethereum, first by building a mining rig, then by authoring the blockchain integration library Web3j, which provides the glue for business applications and Android phones to work with the Ethereum blockchain. The library is nearly five years old and has been downloaded over 1 million times, thanks to usage by companies like J.P. Morgan, Opera and Samsung.

Outside work, when he's not hanging out with his wife and kids, Conor keeps active through a combination of Brazilian jiu-jitsu, running, surfing and stand-up paddle boarding. He also loves sci-fi, fantasy and playing the drums.

He can be found on LinkedIn and Twitter.

in linkedin.com/in/ConorSvensson

🐦 @ConorSvensson